FAITH FOR THESE TROUBLED TIMES

DENSON N. FRANKLIN

FAITH FOR THESE TROUBLED TIMES

FLEMING H. REVELL COMPANY

Westwood, New Jersey
London E.C.4—29 Ludgate Hill
Glasgow C.2—229 Bothwell Street

To my wife
LOTTIE MAE
who has been such an inspiration to me and
who consistently faces each day with faith and confidence

CONTENTS

INTRODUCTION

THIS LITTLE VOLUME is the product of the heart and mind of Denson N. Franklin, who is now finishing his tenth year as pastor of First Methodist Church, Gadsden, Alabama. Dr. Franklin is in the zenith of his middle years, having been admitted into the North Alabama Conference in 1935. He has served small and large churches these twenty-two years. His present pastorate is considered one of the strongest in the Conference. Perhaps one half of his members came into the Church under his ministry.

Preaching is his supreme ambition and joy. Readers will be impressed by the personal and human interest experiences the author has drawn upon to give point to his messages. People, events, and places form his resource material. The Holy Scriptures become luminous in his preaching. The Holy Spirit is not just an "influence" in his life, but has become a living Presence in all situations affecting this pastor's daily ministry. His conclusions are Christ-centered and many are validated by direct quotations from the words of Jesus.

9

Ministers who do counseling with people in distress will find help here. Down-to-earth human problems are dealt with in a way which leads to Christian solutions. Under the influence of these messages, many confused persons will find unity and peace within, and a sense of mission in living through these days.

CLARE PURCELL

I. LIFE IN THESE DAYS

1. WHAT ARE YOU LIVING FOR?

*And all the days of Methuselah were nine hun-
dred sixty and nine years: and he died.*

GENESIS 5:27.

DR. GASTON FOOTE tells about an old man in the Arkansas
Ozark mountains who lived to be one hundred years old.
The newspapers heard about it and sent a reporter and
photographer to interview him and take his picture. The
reporter questioned him about his longevity. The old man
attributed his long life to the fact that he had never tasted
coffee, never smoked, never played golf, never argued with
his wife, and that all his days he had retired religiously at
seven o'clock. Dr. Foote's comment was, "Why he wanted
to live to be one hundred under those circumstances I don't
know."

Several years ago a very close friend of mine got off the

beam in his thinking. He became very selfish. He magnified some of his problems, which were not unlike the kind that others about him were having. He had missed life. The world was against him. He thought about himself day and night. He quit his job and coddled himself. The physician could find little wrong with him except a deep emotional disturbance. He talked of suicide to his parents and friends, until they were worried sick over him. Then one day he came to spend a few hours with me. After my wife had fed us we drifted across to my study at the church and he started to complain. "I'm sick of it all. Life is not worth living. Nobody cares for me. I've come over here today to let you in on a secret. I'm going to kill myself. What do you think about it?" I answered, "Why not?" He turned toward me, his eyes searching my face for some evidence of humor. "What do you mean?" he shouted. "I mean that it seems the only thing you can do. Why live? You have based your life on selfishness. You have forgotten your family, your job, your friends, your responsibilities, and your God. What are you living for?" When I said that he was so angry he could have struck me. He got up and left my study. It distressed me to have to hurt him, but it was necessary. His boasting to so many people that he was planning to kill himself was a certain sign that he didn't intend to. My reaction had shocked him. My question, "What are you living for?" haunted him. In a few days he was back at work, back with his friends, back in his church, and back in the normal path of activities.

The oldest man who ever lived was Methuselah. He lived nine hundred sixty and nine years. It's too bad he didn't live to make it one thousand. I can imagine that on his nine hundred and sixty-ninth birthday he must have walked down into the village and said, "Boys, I have lived nine hundred sixty-nine years." And someone must have answered, "Why?" He probably would have made it to a thousand but for his accidental death. He was living with his grandson, Noah, when God told Noah to build the ark. When God gave a list of the people and animals to save, He neglected to mention Methuselah. When they were recording his life for posterity, there wasn't a single thing they could say. He didn't write a book, he didn't paint a picture, he didn't erect a building, he didn't compose any poetry or music. It could have been said that he was a good gardener, or the best carpenter in the family, or an excellent fisherman; but all that is said is that he lived a long time—and died. Think about the food that he ate. I have been reading, *Captain of the Queens,* by Captain Harry Grattidge, retired captain of the *Queen Mary.* He tells that the *Queen Mary* serves nine thousand meals a day, and on a four-day voyage the passengers and crew consume twelve thousand pounds of ham and butter, five thousand pounds of cheese, sixteen thousand pounds of sugar and seventy-two thousand eggs. How long would that have lasted Methuselah? He must have made the civic clubs and consumed a lot of meat-loaf. Someone has said that if all the meat-loaf he had eaten were laid end to end he would let it lie there! Well, Methuselah lived a long time and ate a long time, but *what did he do?* Now, the father of Methuselah was Enoch. Enoch was a good man and when he was translated the writer said, "And Enoch walked with God and he was not, for God took him." It does not say that Enoch was sick. It does not say that he built a city or became a great artist. He became that which is within the reach of every man. He became a good man and a friend

to God. But his poor son lived until he died. When we read
of his life we are justified in asking the question, "What are
you living for?"

What is your purpose here? What are you goals? Have
you prostituted your talents, lowered your aims, watered
down your convictions? Why are you here?

There are three reasons for which we are challenged to
live: for fellowship, for service and for God.

The words "fellowship" and "friendship" are closely related. We have true fellowship with our friends. We relax
with them. We learn from them. We gain strength through
our fellowship with them. One of the greatest gifts that
God has given mankind is the capacity for friendship.

A prominent minister said that the value of friendship
came home to him in his first pastorate. It was a hard
circuit and the pay was small. He usually owed it all long
before he was paid. But there were many assets. He had the
privilege of serving God and the people, and he had a
friend. The big, gawky, country boy was timid and usually
said the wrong thing when he spoke, but he loved the
preacher, and they became fast friends. The preacher's
mother, who lived with him, became ill and slipped away.
It was a sad day for him—the rain was pouring down, the
parsonage roof was leaking, and his mother was lying in her
coffin in the parlor. There was no food in the cupboard and
the kinsmen were coming soon. Several members of the
congregation called, expressed their sympathy, and went
their way. Then came the gawky country boy. He wouldn't
come in the parlor because his shoes were too muddy, he
said. Instead, he invited the preacher out to the barn, for
he felt at home there and could talk. The preacher walked
with him through the rain, and when they reached the barn

his friend took off his old, wet hat and said, "Now, preacher, I ain't one for talking. I don't know how to express myself about how I feel, but I thought maybe you'd be needin' something and I could do this." He pressed a hundred-dollar bill into the preacher's hand and fled. That meant food and fuel for the parsonage. He was a friend, indeed.

We are reminded of the song, "Don't bring me posies when the shoes is what I need." Sometimes posies are needed, but sometimes shoes are needed more. A friend always knows the difference. Fellowship through friendship is a reason to live.

A second good reason to live is to be able to serve. Great joy comes from serving.

There is a book entitled, *Life Begins at Forty*. Three years ago, when I reached forty, I was tempted to preach a sermon on it. Then I decided that another comment was nearer right—"Life begins to fall apart at forty." But for Moses life really began at forty. It was then that he commenced to serve. Up to then he was a prince possessed of the luxuries of Pharaoh's palace or exiled in the desert, watching his father-in-law's sheep. At forty he saw the burning bush and heard the call to lead his people to the Land of Promise. Life found challenge and adventure. At forty, when he busied himself in serving, he found God and himself.

Albert Schweitzer, in darkest Africa, is an example of a happy, radiant Christian. A man who has mastered several fields and is a graduate in music and medicine, he has given the better part of his life to the jungle people of Equatorial French Africa. One day he was sitting with a helper named Joseph. He decided to test Joseph and said, "Joseph, sometimes I think a man is a fool to throw his life away helping these raw savages." Joseph turned to him and said, "My friend, maybe he is a fool on earth, but surely not in heaven." No man can take the joy of service from Schweitzer.

My thoughts go back to Holguin, Cuba, where 60,000 people live in a sick city without running water or sewerage. I can see our Methodist clinic opening its doors in the early morning to a yard filled with waiting people. I can see them standing in line or sitting on the benches under the trees holding their sick babies. It looks more like ancient Galilee with the people bringing their sick, lame, and blind to Jesus. I can see Dr. Garfield Evans at the door to take the first patient. The face of that seasoned pioneer of Latin American missions is twisted with pain. There is never a moment when he is free of pain. His complexion is dark from the blazing south Cuban sun. As he stands there and looks on the waiting people his pain leaves him momentarily. A smile lights his face. He is serving God and needy humanity. He has a reason to live.

Through our churches we can serve by sending our money to men like this. We can serve by offering to help in Sunday school, Bible school, or on committees organized to send food and clothing to the needy, by working with youth or helping with the Boy and Girl Scouts. There are many ways really to live through service.

The third reason to live is to live for God. Methuselah's father knew the answer to life. Enoch walked with God and had the joy of this holy companionship. Paul knew it, too. He said, "For me to live is Christ." He also said, "I live, yet not I, for Christ liveth in me." Do you want something to live for? Then find Jesus, for He said, "I am the way, the truth and the life." He will give you a reason to live.

Dr. Reuben K. Youngdahl tells of a little boy who often came to a mission school late in the morning. His red eyes and tear-streaked face showed at a glance that he had been crying. One morning the teacher asked, "Why do you cry and why are you often so late?" The boy answered, "My mother doesn't want me to listen to my Jesus-loving teacher. Instead, she wants me to pray to bulls and cows. She hates your God. And when I say I want to go, she only answers, 'You cannot go!' Then she whips me until I cry, but still I want to come. Then finally she says, 'All right, get out of this house and go,' and she does this every morning." The little fellow stood there a moment and then a smile broke through his tears as with grateful eyes he looked at the missionary. Then he said, "But teacher, it is worth it." Yes, it is worth it to live for God. It's worth it to have fellowship with Him. Walking with God gives purpose to life. God gives us something to live for.

2. *KEEPING ALIVE IN THESE DAYS*

*And you he made alive, when you were dead
through the trespasses and sins. . . .*

EPHESIANS 2:1, RSV.

THE EARLY METHODISTS opened their conferences with the
singing of the hymn, "And are we yet alive, and see each
other's face." Theirs was dangerous work. The average age
at death or retirement was in the late thirties and early
forties. It was a real accomplishment to be alive at conference time after facing the wilderness and the tests of
pioneer preaching. But there one thing was certain—they
were spiritually alert and alive.

A little boy wrote a letter to his father who had gone
to war. He had heard enough around the house to know
something of the dangers his father faced and that he might
never return. His heart was filled with anxiety and fear. In

his own way he expressed himself to his father. He wrote, "I hope that you will be alive as long as you live."

Some of us are living dead men. This seems like a paradox, but it isn't. We are alive in some respects and dead in others. There was the story of the old man who was too lazy to live. Eating was too much trouble and working was out of the question. His neighbors decided to go ahead and bury him, since he wouldn't feed himself. They purchased a casket and put him in it. Down the road went the strange funeral procession. A traveling salesman calling at the village store looked up and saw the procession. The old man sat up in the coffin and looked around as his neighbors bore him to his final resting place. The salesman asked the merchant what was going on, then rushed into the street to intercept the procession. He came up to the old man in the casket and said, "You must not be buried now. I have a sack of corn I'll give you to eat." The old man rubbed his chin whiskers and said, "Is it shelled?" "No, it isn't." "Then march on to the cemetery, boys," said the old man. So many people are dead over trifles.

When I was a boy our store had a customer out in the country who thought a lot about death. He was an old bachelor, had no family responsibilities, no wife to argue with and be petted by—he was absolutely alone. He had his grave dug and bought his coffin. The coffin stood on the back porch near the well shelter, leaning against the wall. I tell you, when we had to deliver goods out there I was scared within an inch of my life. When the poor fellow finally gave up the ghost he had gained so much weight that they couldn't get him in his own coffin. Mentally and spiritually, however, he had died years before his heart stopped beating.

One day at a preachers' meeting we were making our weekly reports. One preacher got up and said, "This has been a terrible week in my church. Two of my stewards have died." Another preacher, who was quite a wit, stood and said, "It's always a bad week for me. I have twenty stewards who are dead and don't know it."

Paul, in his letter to the church in Ephesus, lifts up Christ as the Redeemer of mankind and the Giver of life. A theologian had been asked to give his opinion of the power of Billy Graham and he answered, "I think his power is found in his message on Jesus Christ. Christ is always at the heart of his messages." That was Paul's power, too. Writing to the church in Ephesus, he reminded them of what had happened. They had been walking dead men, dead in trespasses and sins—mere ghosts of themselves. Hopeless men, helpless men, dead men. Christ had quickened them. He had given them life. Sin destroys. Sin is the master of destruction. Sin brings death, but Christ is the emancipator. When we are dead in trespasses and sins, in prejudices and hate, in envy and strife, in our sinful appetites, He comes to bring life, for He said, "I am the resurrection and the life."

Do you want to stay alive? Dr. Joseph Fort Newton said that there are three essentials for real living: a faith fit to live by, a self fit to live with, and a work fit to live for. These three are the main clauses in a life insurance policy. Let us look at them, in a different order, as a trilogy on life.

It is essential to have a self fit to live with. You can run away from everybody but yourself, and you can fool everybody but yourself. One of the prime factors in internal dis-

turbances is self-hate. We testify, "I have let myself down.
I have sold myself out. I am no good."

Isaiah went to the temple with his troubles. What he saw
wasn't a pretty picture. He saw the Lord; then he saw
himself. He saw how undone he was, how sinful—and he
did something about it.

It's hard to look at yourself. Some of us can stand looking
at other people but we just can't look at ourselves. Much
gossip actually is condemnation of others in order to cover
up our own weaknesses that we don't want to admit. Someone has said, "The reason we like a dog so well is that he
wags his tail instead of his tongue." And another said, "The
only person who can be successful at running people down
is the elevator boy."

Gypsy Smith used to tell of a man who would not look
at himself. He professed to be religious but actually his
family couldn't stand him. They wouldn't even go to the
same church with him. Then one day his preacher said in
a sermon that everyone should take a piece of chalk, draw
a circle, get into it, and ask God to help him see himself.
This man did that and was transformed. When his wife
and daughter came in from the church across town, they
saw him standing, with tears of repentance in his eyes,
in the circle which he had made on the living-room rug.
They asked him to make the circle larger and let them
get in.

Are you fit to live with? A man seventy-five years of age
went to his doctor for a check-up. The doctor found him
perfectly well. He said, "I have never seen a man your age
in better condition. What kind of exercise have you taken?"
The old man said, "When my wife and I married fifty
years ago we made an agreement that if we should ever get

into a serious fuss over the house, or the in-laws, or money, or anything like that, she would keep on working in the house and I would take a long walk out-of-doors. Well, sir, I guess my good health must be due to the fact that for the last fifty years I have lived pretty much of an outdoor life." Are you making life miserable for your wife, your husband, parents, friends? Are you making life miserable for yourself? Are you unhappy, fuming, fussing, grumbling about something all the time? The poet has expressed it:

> If I had the time to find a place
> And sit me down full face to face,
> With me and my better self,
> I'm sure that life would be sublime,
> If I had the time.

We can stay alive if we have a self fit to live with.

A work fit to live for keeps you from dying. A work fit to keep you busy, keeps you alive. Two years ago I went back to my first Conference appointment, in the mining district, to hold a meeting. One day I dined with Brother Sharp Calhoun, a faithful member of the church and faithful employee of the Woodward Iron Company. He had retired a few months before but couldn't stay away from the mines. He was up early and in the machine shop every morning. His wife thought it strange. He said to me, "Brother Franklin, I can't help it. For forty years I have given my life to that work. I love it. I feel that they need me. No retirement law can keep me away from there."

Michelangelo meant well when he said, "It is well with me only when I have a chisel in my hand." Our happiest moments are those when we lose ourselves in a great task. Work is not a penalty for sin—it is a blessing. There is the old story of the two men at work on a cathedral. When someone asked them what they were doing, one said, "I'm making a day's pay." But the other stopped, put down his tools, pointed to the walls of the great church, and said, "I am building a cathedral."

The word "vocation" is coming into its own again. Elton Trueblood has rightly reminded us that it is not only the priests who take holy orders. All who regard their particular work as a means of serving God and humanity are under holy orders.

When Nehemiah was building the walls around Jerusalem, the renegade Sanballat did his best to draw him from his work to the plains of Ono. Nehemiah answered, "I am doing a great work, so I cannot come down." That is a good word to shout to evil—"I'm doing a great work and I cannot compromise my standards and prostitute my aims."

Jesus made work sacred. He talked about a farmer planting seed, a carpenter building a house, a shepherd tending his sheep, a commercial fisherman at work. He blessed the work of man and made it a sacred rite at God's altar. If we turn it over to Him He will bless it, and the efforts of our hands will find praise in His sight.

If you want to stay alive you must have a faith to live by. G. K. Chesterton used to tell of a landlady who put only one question to prospective boarders. It was this: "What is your view of the universe?" She did not inquire about a man's personal habits, or the kind of company he kept. She asked what he believed. She was right. She knew that you know a person when you know what he believes. Belief shapes the pattern of a life.

Some time ago I had a private conference with Dr. Roy Burkhart, pastor of the First Community Church, Columbus,

Ohio. To spend an hour with him is worth a long journey. He is a great counselor and friend. When you listen to him you feel that he is filled with the Holy Spirit. He talks quietly of faith which can remove mountains and cast them into the midst of the sea. He speaks of dynamic spiritual power that comes from above, and the witness of the spirit in the human heart which overcomes fear, anxiety, and even physical fatigue. It is a faith that takes away the anemic Christian living that characterizes most of us and in its place puts vigor and spiritual stamina.

One day I accompanied a pastor to see a dying man in the hospital in another community. The pastor explained that this was one of the best men he knew; that even eaten up with cancer and on his deathbed, he was more alive than most of his flock. We went into the room. The dying man was under an oxygen tent. He had his nurse unzip it and asked me to put my head down to the opening so that we could talk. The deep faith, the radiance, the bubbling over with life that this man had, put me to shame. Shame because I am well and have more to give physically. In his presence I was paled into insignificance. He was almost dead physically, but alert and alive in spirit.

Thanks be unto God that when we are dead in trespasses and sins we have a God who can make us live and keep us alive in these days.

3. TOMORROW MAY BE TOO LATE—
TODAY MUST COUNT

> . . . when I have a convenient season, I will
> call for thee.   ACTS 24:25.

SOME MONTHS AGO I saw a movie which, because of its deep
religious implications and teachings, might well have been
shown in any church. It was entitled, "Come Next Spring."
The setting was in the Ozark mountains following World
War I, amid the joys, sorrows, hardships and pleasures of
that period and place. The theme was taken from an
expression so often heard in conversation—"come next
spring." Come next spring, we'll plant a better crop than
this one. Come next spring, we'll build a better house, or
we'll make peace with our neighbors; we'll forgive our
enemies, we'll give up our bad habits, we'll start going to
church. Yes, without much effort it will all work out some-

29

where in the vague, distant future. It will all work out,
come next spring.

Jesus saw this human trait and tried to cope with it. He
saw people putting off responsibility and sleeping through
one experience after another. He told the parable of the
ten virgins. He said that the kingdom of heaven was likened
unto ten virgins which took their lamps and went forth to
meet the bridegroom. Five of them were foolish and five
were wise. They that were foolish took no oil with them,
but the wise took extra oil in their vessels. While the bridegroom tarried they all slumbered and slept. The foolish
virgins who were about to exhaust their supply of oil slept
on. They said, "It will work out somehow. Come the time,
we'll get more oil." So they slept. Then the cry went out,
"The bridegroom cometh, go ye out to meet him." The five
wise virgins were ready to go with their lamps and ample
supply of oil, but the foolish sought the shops to buy more
oil. When they returned the ceremony was going on, and
the door was shut. The doorkeeper answered their calls,
"I know you not."

After the Apostle Paul was arrested in Jerusalem under
false charges, he was carried to Cæsarea to the seat of the
Roman government to be tried by Felix, the governor. Paul
refuted the charge against him and then proceeded to
preach to Felix. "And as he reasoned of righteousness, tem-
perance and judgment to come, Felix trembled, and
answered, Go thy way for this time; when I have a convenient season, I will call for thee." He was saying, "Come
next spring, and maybe I'll do something about it. I'll find a
convenient place out yonder somewhere and I'll make a
decision."

There are many Felixes in the world. And there is a

certain amount of Felix in all of us. That is why some wise man said, "Never put off until tomorrow what you can do today."

You remember the story of the old hermit who had such a bad leak in his roof? Someone asked him why he didn't fix it, and his answer was, "When the sun is shining and the weather is fair it doesn't need fixing, and when it's pouring rain it's too wet to fix." There is the Felix in all of us. We are bad about putting off unpleasant encounters or demanding situations. Indeed, "procrastination is the thief of time," and it is also a thief of character and of faith. Watering the cow and bringing in the wood always brought out the Felix in me. I would put off. I would try to steal some time. That cow could drink more water than an elephant, and the well was deep. Besides that, the woodbox by the fireplace and the other back of the kitchen stove were always empty. Now, there's nothing in the world that looks quite so empty as an empty woodbox. Maybe there is an old dry chip in it or a piece of bark. I don't think I ever saw those woodboxes full. I used to dream of growing up and inventing a machine which you could just crank up and run a belt on it to the woodshed to bring in the wood. And that old cow! Well, I almost quit drinking milk, because I had no use for her at all. Night would come and I would still be daydreaming, hoping and praying that an angel would fill the woodboxes and water the cow. But the angel never came. Like the man at the Pool of Bethesda who waited thirty-eight years for the angel to ripple the water, I waited thirty-eight minutes for the same angel; but strangely, the angel never came, and darkness always found me pushing like mad to fill the woodboxes and water that cow.

As grown people, mature adults, we use a different language; but we still have the Felix in us.

It's good to be a booster of your community. An old fellow was whittling in front of a store in a little town, when a big car drove up. The driver called out, "We're looking for a nice place to live. Do people live very long here?" "Oh, yes, sir," the old-timer answered, "they never die here." "Well," said the stranger, "I don't understand. I just saw a funeral procession turn to go into the cemetery outside of town." The old man thought a moment and then said, "Oh, that—that was our local undertaker. The poor fool starved to death." That is the way to boost your town. The time comes, though, when you must face the issues that plague your community. There is the temptation to wait for next spring to work them out.

That goes for our schools and our problem concerning the education of our youth. It goes for the juvenile delinquency rate that continues to climb and keeps us all worried. Next spring may be too late.

That can happen to the churches of a community, too. Last year I held a revival in a community in Alabama where this had happened. The pastor told me that none of the churches was reaching the young people. The members in control of the policies of the churches had refused to allow any change from the approach of their fathers. Youth suppers and recreation were not allowed in the church basement. Youth choirs were opposed. Who wanted to hear them? Said he, "The great pay-off has come now. The churches are losing in membership. The young people have married and are not bringing their children to Sunday school and church. Every funeral now is another death blow to our churches, because no one comes to take the vacant place." There was no excitement in our revival. I felt called of God to present the facts to the people in the church in which I was holding the revival. I read the funeral ritual to them, so to speak. At first I drew anger, but it turned out to be one of the best revivals I ever held—people came to see God's plan. They gave up their selfishness. One prominent woman said, "You have helped me to see how wrong I have been in my opposition to a youth program. I have offered my services to our pastor and have asked his forgiveness, too. We are going to work here and you can count on that." Once they sang, "On Jordan's Stormy Banks I Stand," while the young people and the masses of the community were singing, "Drifting Down the River on a Sunday Afternoon."

We are apt to put off the development of good habits— I'm going to change my way of living, next spring. But the Felix in me tells me to wait for a more convenient season. I'm going to be more thoughtful, come next spring. I've been too busy, but one day I am going to start being more considerate of loved ones and others.

I had a roommate who never wrote his mother. I have made a practice of writing my mother once a week but he fiddled away his time and would never write. When he would see me taking my letter to mail, the tears would come in his eyes and he would say, "I'm going to turn over a new leaf soon. My precious mother has been so good to me. I'm going to start next week." But he never did.

Husband, when are you going to be more thoughtful? When have you carried your wife a box of candy or some flowers? Much of my work is counseling, and I can't afford to share experiences with anyone, not even my dear mate of the years; but when I turn over a new leaf once in a

while and bring her a gift she will smile and say, "Boy, you
have had a family problem today, I just know." Turn over
a new leaf. With some of us the same old leaf grows yellow
and faded—we don't try any more.

And, wife, what about you? I have known wives who
have stayed in bed all day reading a romance, so that when
the husband came home the beds were still unmade, the
dinner not prepared, the house in disorder. Romance? You
can't expect much love from your mate when you act like
that. Let the home be cheerful, alive, vibrant with love.

Some of us plan to drop a bad habit, come next spring.
We are going to give up drinking next spring. Then there
was the man who had promised to quit drinking but never
got around to it. He was a "take-it-or-leave-it" fellow; he
just took it. So the family planned for him. One Saturday
night he came home drunk, so they carried him to the
cemetery and buried him, all but his head. When he came
to himself on Sunday morning he was there in the cemetery.
The birds were singing and the sun was shining. He shouted,
"Resurrection morning and I'm the first one up!"

Some of us are going to right old wrongs, come next
spring. We are going to give flowers to our neglected
friends, come next spring. We are going to make peace
with our enemies, come next spring. But, usually, next
spring never comes. It is always the long, bleak winter.
Today should be the day of spring.

Many of us have the tendency to put off our search for
spiritual peace. There was a man who wanted to follow
Jesus some time in the future, but, first, he wanted to return
home and bury his father. His father was getting on in
years and the son wanted to remain with him until the end.
Come next spring, he would follow Jesus. The Master said,

"Follow me; and let the dead bury their dead." The young man turned away; he wanted to wait.

Felix heard Paul's arguments. They impressed the Roman governor. His heart was warmed, but he wanted more time. His conscience would not let him fully reject Paul's teaching. He compromised by making a vague promise to himself and to Paul. "When I have a convenient season I will call for thee." Out yonder somewhere I'll work it out, he was saying. Give me time. But so far as we know, he never got around to it.

There is a legend that Satan called a meeting of his imps and said, "You are all wrong in the way you are trying to refute the Christian gospel. Tell them that God is real and they should trust Him. Tell them that the gospel is true, that Christ died for them. But tell them not to be in a hurry. They have plenty of time." Procrastination is the thief of time; it is also a thief of souls. There is a point on the Niagara river, I am told, which is called "Point Beyond Redemption." There is a chance to pull one's boat to shore before it reaches a certain point, but beyond that, where the turbulent waters approach the falls, there is a point where control of the boat is lost completely. There is nothing left to do but go over. There is a point in the affairs of men where one's spiritual destiny is out of his hands. We do not know where that point is or how soon or late we reach it. It may even be at the last moment of consciousness, but no one should toy with the idea that he will reach it safely. Don't put off concern for your soul until you have lost interest and are caught in the swift waters of indifference.

A painting in a European art gallery depicted a boy and the devil playing chess. The devil had the boy cornered.

No matter what move he made the devil could sweep him from the board. The cunning look of satisfaction in the devil's face reveals that the game was nearly over. One day a party came to the gallery and one member remained behind, while the others moved on. When the others returned he was still standing before this painting in deep study. Hours passed and he would not leave. Finally, just as the closing time came and the guards warned him that he must leave, the man shouted, "I can take the boy's place and beat the devil at his own game." He was the world's champion chess player. Christ is the champion of life and death and the victor in the affairs of men. He can take man's place and beat the devil at his own game. Don't neglect your faith. Accept Christ now as your Saviour. Come next spring may be too late.

II. THE PROBLEMS OF THESE DAYS

4. TAPROOTS FOR THE STORMS OF THE DAY

> ... and because they had no root, they withered away.   MATTHEW 13:6.

> If the foundations be destroyed, what can the righteous do?   PSALM 11:3.

Do YOU HAVE something to hold to in these stormy days? Do you have a firm foundation which can withstand the blasts of the tempest? That is a question which every man needs to answer down in his soul.

Some time ago I read *Street of Knives*, by Cyril Harris. It is the story of Aaron Burr. Squire Blennerhassett had lost his island estate to follow Burr. Burr had been arrested and the whole plot exposed. There on the flat boat anchored in the Mississippi River, the Squire was a dejected man.

He thought the whole world had gone to pot. He stood, leaning on the rail looking into the water, when another member of his party, Hugh, came up. "Lost something, Squire?" he asked. "Aye, Hugh, that I have," came the answer. He hesitated a moment then answered, "Hugh, do you see this handrail? I'm leaning on it and you are, too. That's what I've lost—the handrail. Something to hold me back when I get too near the edge. It has to be strong and it has to be there. Men call it God. I'm looking for it."

A few days ago I turned through the pages of another book which I had read some years earlier, *Tap Roots,* by James Street. It's the story of the Dabney family who lived in the free state of Lebanon in South Mississippi during the War between the States. The author states that similar circumstances did exist in that state during the war, although the characters in the book are fictitious. The Dabneys rebelled against the Confederacy. They argued that it was their land, their homes, even their lives that they were fighting for, that they would do what they wanted to. It's a bloody story of the efforts of the Confederacy to subdue the Dabney clan; and an equally beautiful story of their love for the land and for their traditions. They had their roots down and intended to stay there.

Men must have a handrail to lean on—to keep them from falling into the water, as the Squire so aptly put it. They must have roots that go down deep into the soil of tradition, culture, beliefs—to hold when the storms of life assail them. They must have foundations on which to build their lives.

Jesus understood that. No man who ever lived better understood human personality than did Christ. He was concerned for men that they have something which would hold up. One day a large multitude came to hear Him. He talked from a seat in a boat so that He might address the entire congregation standing on the shore. He used a vivid illustration, with the farmer as the chief character. A sower went forth to sow. Some seeds fell by the way and the fowls came and devoured them. Some seeds fell in stony places, where they had not much earth. Because the soil was shallow they sprang up immediately. But when the hot sun came out they were scorched, and because they had no root they withered away. Others were choked by thorns, and others fell into good ground, developed roots, and brought forth much fruit. Those which had no roots couldn't stand the test. Those which had roots grew. That is a law of life. You must have depth of rootage to stand the tests of life.

The Psalmist said practically the same, yet expressed it in a different way. Said he, "If the foundations be destroyed, what can the righteous do?"

Man must have a handrail to lean on; he must have a firm grasp of it to withstand the storms which beat on him.

Ours is a shallow generation. Many of our frustrations may be traced to our inclination to live on the surface. Veneer, sham, pretense, are words that indicate our shallowness. We try to appear calm, balanced, poised, on the surface, but down underneath we have nothing.

Bishop John Wesley Lord at Lake Junaluska, North Carolina, spoke of Queen Victoria's visit to one of the colonies. Her reign during the latter half of the nineteenth century was one of great prosperity and progress in the British Empire. Everywhere she went her subjects tried too hard to impress her. When she would visit a community in the colony the workmen would rush ahead, cover the bad spots with greenery, flowers, and transplanted trees. Then, when she started her journey to another village, they would take up the scenery and rush it ahead to that village. A native who saw them moving the trees about said, "They don't want their trees to have roots." That, too, is a condemnation of our twentieth century. We don't want our lives to have roots. We prefer sham, pretense, veneer.

In 1952 I enjoyed my visit to the studios of Twentieth Century Fox in Hollywood. Two of us, with our guide, saw the sets for "The Song of Bernadette." It was like walking through an abandoned French village. Then we passed on to a town set up for Western pictures. It gave me a peculiar feeling to be out there in a regular Western village, with only the three of us, not a sound anywhere, not a voice, not a person. There was the depot and standing before it the old train, engine and two coaches. We walked down the dusty streets. There were the hitching posts and the water troughs. I stood there in amazement. The buildings lining the street were weather-beaten. On one side was the old hotel, and next door the saloon with the swinging doors. Next to that, Mrs. Cook's boardinghouse, with the big sign, "Meals 15¢—Bed and Breakfast 25¢." At the end of the street was the little white church with its simple spire. There was the Wells-Fargo office and the stage coach in front. I couldn't feel safe in the streets to save me. I kept looking for some cowboys to ride into town and run me down. Then I said to the guide, "This is as real as anything I have ever seen in my life. It's like going back to the old days of the wild and woolly West." Then I walked over to Mrs. Cook's boardinghouse, went up on the porch, opened the door, and started in. Then I got my shock. The whole interior was made up of brace timbers holding up the outside walls. It was just veneer. The guide got a big kick out of it. He explained that only the outside was needed, therefore why go to the expense of furnishing the inside? He was exactly right. But when it comes to a life—that is different. We must have something on the inside to back up our outside appearance. The trouble is, we are a generation of false fronts, our lives have no depth.

Some years ago the dikes of Holland broke under the lashing of a terrific storm, and the sea poured in on the land. One hundred thousand people were driven from their homes. Nothing was left to them except what they carried away on their backs or in their carts. In three months, however, they returned to the same land which for centuries had been at the mercy of storm and wind. Why did they? Their forefathers had lived there. It was their home. Their roots were deep in the land.

Some of our frustration comes from being uprooted by war, or by changing communities and leaving behind our roots. But more of it comes from our changing habits, customs, standards, morals, convictions. Some of the most frustrated people I have known are people who have forsaken the old ways for new paths that they do not relish.

Let me illustrate. In a hospital for nerve disorders a few years ago was a woman I came to know about. The psychiatrists delved deep into her case. They could find nothing physically wrong. The trouble was in her mind and soul. They finally found it. She had lost her rootage. She had been reared in a Christian home, but had married a man who had built his life around social affairs. Religion was taboo in their house. They never darkened the doors of a church. The name of God was supposed not to be even whispered except to take it in vain. Their life was one

drunken party after another; morals were thrown aside
as antiquated. She had become confused. She had no handrail to lean on, and had torn away from the roots of her
Christian background. Confusion and frustration brought
on a breakdown.

Our lives must be rooted in the soil of faith. In one of his
earlier books Leslie Weatherhead tells of a vine which grew
on a wall of his compound during his stay in India. One
night, during the monsoon season, the apparently well-
fortified wall collapsed. Weatherhead could not understand
it. He went out to examine the wall. To his surprise, he
found it literally full of roots. The plant had slowly but
surely permeated the wall with its tiny roots and then
tightened up so as to destroy the wall easily. If roots can
destroy like that, they can also do the almost impossible
in strengthening and holding in the worst storms.

Social and political storms are sweeping the world today.
Old institutions are crumbling; old ways of life are being
discarded. Great tidal waves of ideologies move across the
globe, engulfing people and nations. Do you have your
roots down deep?

When President Syngman Rhee served notice on the
United Nations that he would not be bound by any armis-
tice which would jeopardize the independence of his
country, the pot began to boil in all the countries involved.
The whole world was astir over this matter. Former Am-
bassador Bullitt reports that he was resting at a mountain
retreat with President Rhee during this time. What did
Syngman Rhee talk about? International affairs, politics,
the fate of his people? No! He spoke rather of faith, of
God, of the things which give a man quiet and strength
in these disturbing times. In the social and political storm

that swept the world he had something to hold to. In the hour of great crisis for his country this little Methodist steward, Christian, and statesman, had his roots deep down in the soil of faith.

There are storms which beat on moral convictions. During World War II a young flyer, S. A. Constantine, Jr., who was located at the base in Pensacola, Florida, wrote a little book entitled, *Amen—Amen.* It is a straight-from-the-shoulder approach to a problem that all servicemen face, the problem of temptation and the breaking down of moral standards. The author faces squarely the loneliness of a man away from home, and the tests which come when a man is jerked out of his job, his home, and his circle of friends, to a sort of life which he has known little about. Constantine doesn't dodge anything. The road is not an easy one. But the flyer comes to the conclusion that background and childhood training pay off here. Only the men who have strong foundations have survived the trials of temptation. Shouldn't this be a challenge to every home? Shouldn't it make a father and mother more careful in their lives before their children? Some children do exceptionally well when you consider their rootage. Their parents have lived on the surface. They have forsaken the house of the Lord, and have lived like animals before their children. Their lives influence their offspring. Tragedies come to the children as a result of the parents' carelessness. *Foundations are important.*

There are storms of the soul. We need strength to face victory and defeat and take them both in stride, to learn from each its costly message, to face the stresses and strains of everyday living, and death itself. The roots make the difference.

The home, the school, the church, each has a great job —to plant the seeds of truth deep in soil made fertile by love and care so that our children will have proper foundation and rootage for life.

I had just moved to a new church. Among the new people I had met, one face was missing. That person had attended a church college, had been licensed to preach, and had served a circuit for one year. I had expected him to be one of the first to greet me, since he now lived in this neighborhood. His friends were slow to answer my questions. Finally, one told me where he lived, but that he never came to church. He had become embittered and had quit the church. I went to see him. He was most unhappy to see me. The baby was being put to bed and my presence seemed to be disturbing. I turned to go, when he beckoned me to wait. When the baby was placed in her crib, he took me out on the porch and said, "I'm glad you have come. I had hoped you wouldn't, but I'm glad you have. I've been out of sorts and away from God. Life has been miserable for me. You know, I was brought up in a Christian home. I have the best mother and father that anybody could have. They taught me the right things. I'm like the Psalmist when he said, 'As the hart panteth after the water brooks, so panteth my soul after thee, O God.' I'm thirsty to come back. I'm going to come back. My roots are down deep in the soil of faith. They won't turn me loose." He came back and became one of the best men I had in my church for the four years I was there. His rootage was secure. Do you have that? If not, today is a good time to plant the seed of faith in Christ.

5. EXCESS BAGGAGE MUST GO— NOW

> *. . . let us lay aside every weight, and the sin*
> *which doth so easily beset us . . . Looking unto*
> *Jesus the author and finisher of our faith. . . .*
> HEBREWS 12:1-2.

A MAN WHOSE life was burdened far beyond the weight human strength could endure was contemplating suicide, when on the wall of a railway station he saw these words: "Let Go—Let God." The text and this motto will guide our thought in this chapter.

The date and authorship of the Epistle to the Hebrews are unknown. Certain evidence makes it fairly clear that it was written before the destruction of the Temple in Jerusalem in 70 A.D. While some believe that St. Paul wrote it, John Calvin regarded St. Luke as the author. Luther be-

lieved Apollos to be the writer, and other eminent com-
mentators attribute it to Barnabas. But one thing is certain,
the author knew a great deal about two subjects—life and
God. He lived in an era which was familiar with the great
athletic events of the Roman Empire. Men of might met
before huge crowds to compete for mastery. One of the
events was the race. People by the thousands came in from
the towns and villages to the Roman cities to see mighty
runners compete for the trophy. In Hebrews, the writer
compared life to a race. The runner has a great host of
witnesses who follow his every move. His goal is Jesus
Christ, the author and finisher of our faith. If he is to win
he must let go of anything which might delay or interfere
with his progress. He cannot do his best in the race when
he is bound or weighed down—he must be free of excess
baggage. The Christian life is like that. We must lay aside
every weight and the sin which doth so easily beset us, and
run with patience. It is a matter of letting go and letting
God.

There are some things which we must remember in these
days.

You can't escape life. Some years ago, at the beginning
of World War II, I read a newspaper article which stated
that a prominent businessman of the Pacific Northwest was
selling his business and moving with his two young daughters to the wilderness—far from "the crowded ways of life."
He said that life had become too complicated and that he
chose no longer to run the race. With his two daughters, he
chose the rôle of the hermit. In the wilderness he would
teach them, and there the three would live forever in
peace. I do not know how the noble experiment turned out,
but I can make a safe guess.

One night at a Sunday-school meeting in one of my pastorates, I heard a huge plane flying low over the church. I had a feeling that the sky monster was in trouble. Then the call came back to the town for ambulances. A B-29 had crashed north of town. As a minister of the gospel I joined the first group to go to the scene of the accident. Some twelve or fourteen people aboard the plane had been blown to bits. It was a night of horror—the burning plane and the burning flesh. Fires burned caused by the debris from the exploding plane in places along a two-mile path. A Negro farmer told of having seen the crash. He was on his way to the barn to milk his cow when this great monster came out of the sky, spitting fire. It struck some pine trees across the road from him and exploded. He said, "I'se heard about these big airplanes, but way back up here in the country I never expected to see one. A man can't find a safe place these days." He was right. You can't run from life.

You know the song that was popular some time ago: "Oh, you'll never get away—never get away—never get away—never get away—never get away." How true, you'll never get away. You've got to face life.

We went down to Daytona Beach, Florida, before World War II to "get away." War clouds were slowly shaping over the world. We wanted to hear the roar of the surf and to smell the salt breeze, and forget it all. We had no reservations, so we tried several places. It was late and we were tired. Finally, in one hotel the manager said that during the Fourth of July season we would never find anything, for nothing was open in town, but that he would let us use his room until the next morning, when he would have an opening for us. It was a stuffy, hot, little back room, but we were so exhausted that it didn't matter. We fell asleep in a moment. I thought as I lay down, "How wonderful! No worries, no troubles, no war, just rest and a vacation." Then I had a horrible experience. I suddenly awakened. My body was stiff and taut as a banjo string. I heard a voice, low and mysterious, say, "Europe shall be bathed in blood. Her beaches shall be piled high with the carnage of war and human wreckage. Millions shall be homeless and hundreds of thousands shall die." I saw a dim light under the door. I tiptoed over to the door and listened. A spiritualist medium was holding a séance in the next room. I thought I had gotten away from troubles and here was trouble right next door. *You can't run away.*

Someone must take the lead and face the bullets fired at leadership in a restless age.

Nation magazine had an article, June 18, 1949, entitled, "Ulcers and History." We were shocked to learn how much leadership cost today, Many public leaders and world leaders develop ulcers because of the strain. Think how that in a few short years many of these men are dead or retired. We sometimes worry about young men getting into high office in this country. If we don't use them in their thirties and forties and fifties, where are we going to get leaders? We kill them or retire them under pressure of bad health in a few years. Responsibility is a fearful thing. You can't run away from it.

In *The Sage of Walden Pond,* Thoreau said, "I went to the woods because I wished to live deliberately." He complained about the mad race of man at thirty miles per hour. But the strain of living has forced man from his quiet pond out into the hubbub of a fast-moving world. And you can't run away from it.

If we would face the tests of living, we must lay aside the weight of our sins as excess baggage.

Tension interferes with the face of life. After spending six months in bed, David Grayson wrote, "Nowhere with more freedom from trouble does a man retire than in his own soul." Also, "Tranquility is nothing else than the good ordering of the mind." Good ordering involves keeping calm in mind and spirit while busy in body.

To feel slighted is a commonplace with many of us. How many times have you gotten your feelings hurt this month? Someone slighted you or made a "catty" remark about you. It burned like a fire in your bosom. Some people will hurt you if they can. They get satisfaction out of it. It is a sickness with them. Then some of us have a "martyr complex." We go about saying, "I'm a door mat, please step on me." We stay hurt all the time and get a lot of joy out of being hurt. You know the old saying, "Don't put your big feet in the aisle if you don't want the conductor to step on them."

When the colossal statue of Christ of the Andes was erected on the borders between Argentina and Chile years ago, it was created of melted bullets that symbolized the end of a long and bloody strife. When certain Chileans noticed that the Christ faced Argentina the war almost started anew. Rumors flew across the country. "The people of Argentina have slighted us," the Chileans would say. "They have taken advantage of us." Then a wise man started a new rumor to refute that one. He said, "Why, that is the greatest compliment that can be paid us. He has His back on Chile for He trusts us. He is gazing out toward Argentina because they need watching." This rumor caused a tidal wave of laughter across the nation.

Some time ago a speaker told of a barefoot boy of four

who was walking along one hot summer day eating an ice-cream cone, when suddenly a gang of older boys came along and knocked the lad down, spilling his ice cream. The little fellow sat up and surveyed the tragedy. A wise old lady had seen the whole thing from her porch. She came out and said, "Well, son, the very worst has happened to you. But stand up and I will show you something." The little fellow got to his feet. "Now, you put your foot on top of your ice cream and step hard. Doesn't it feel good?" she asked. They watched the cool, yellow ice cream come right up through his toes. They both chuckled. "I'll bet," she said, "there isn't a boy in this town who has ever had his toes cooled with ice cream. Now run home and tell your mother. Remember, whatever happens in life, there is usually a funny side, too."

Oh, you say, that may be so with ice cream, but take my case. It is different. Before you make up your mind read Addison's "Spectator," Number 26, "When I see Kings lying by those who disposed of them, when I consider holy men that divided the world with their contests and disputes placed side by side, I reflect with sorrow and astonishment on the little competitions, factions, and debates of mankind. When I read the several dates on the tombs, of some that died yesterday and some six hundred years ago, I consider *that* great day when we shall all of us be contemporaries and make an appearance together." Where will my little hurt feelings and grievances be then?

The writer of Hebrews said, "Let us lay aside every weight and the sin which doth so easily beset us, looking unto Jesus." That is the gist of the message to be learned from the well-known motto, "Let Go—Let God," which the man saw on the wall of the depot when he contemplated suicide because he felt swamped by his trouble. He let go and let God lead his life. We can't avoid life with its problems. We can trust God to help us with them. When we have done our best we can leave our troubles and problems in God's hands. He does all things well. Life is taking a step at a time.

Dr. Roy Smith tells that one evening during his boyhood in Kansas his father asked him to go to the harness shed and bring back a piece of harness. The lad went to the door and saw the pitch blackness outside. He started crying, "I'm afraid of the dark, daddy." The father gave him the lantern and said, "Now go, son." "But, father, I can see only a little ahead of me with the lantern." "That is the way it is, son: you can hold high the lantern and see one step at a time. But as you walk, you can always see another step ahead." The lad took the lantern and, by taking one step at a time, made the journey to the shed and back. Life is like that. When we let go, God takes us one step at a time.

Amid his troubles, Cardinal Newman soon found that one step is enough, as is indicated in the words of that great hymn:

> Lead, kindly light, amid the encircling gloom,
>   Lead Thou me on!
> The night is dark, and I am far from home;
>   Lead Thou me on!
> Keep Thou my feet: I do not ask to see
> The distant scene; one step enough for me.

6. FACING THE CONFLICTS OF THIS HOUR

If it be possible, as much as lieth in you, live peaceably with all men. ROMANS 12:18.

A soft answer turneth away wrath: but grievous words stir up anger. PROVERBS 15:1.

CONFLICT IS AS real as this universe itself. Every human being who lives on this globe is subject to the multiplied irritations of life which tense our nerves and exhaust our bodies. Conflict and confusion vary according to one's job, neighbors, and the city or village where he lives. But no man is removed from this experience. Whether one will admit it or not, conflict and confusion play a big part in everyday living.

Dr. Hans Selye, Professor of Experimental Medicine at

the University of Montreal, has given some startling information from his experiments. He used some rats in an experiment of conflict. He placed them in a good cage. They were given the best food, but they were constantly worried. A dog stood outside their glass cage and growled and threatened them while they ate. Loud noises were produced in all sorts of ways. Now and then a heavy object was dropped on their cage. In a short time the rats were worn out, although they had not been physically hurt. Conflict had taken its toll.

In life there are many conflicts which irritate us almost beyond human endurance. This is a real problem in living.

Conflict may be divided into two kinds: conflict with people, and conflict with our material world.

Unfortunately, in life we cannot get our conflict with people over at one time and have done with it. It occurs all through life where personalities meet and opinions are expressed. It would be well if only we could follow the custom of a Kaffir tribe. This African tribe has an interesting wedding custom. The ceremony takes all day. Some time during the day the bride will rise up and break into a rage against the man she is marrying. She screams, accuses, and denounces the groom with every evil name she can remember. He is the ugliest man she has ever seen. He is selfish. His mother should have drowned him when he was a boy. It makes her sick to look at him. She wonders why any girl with the sense of a pig would ever consent to marry him. He is a stupid ox. This tantrum is a part of the ceremony, but after the marriage the wife is supposed not to talk back or act meanly to her husband. She is allowed to get it all out of her system before marriage begins!

In one college I attended my fraternity held an annual ceremony. After the opening of school, the pledging and acceptance, when the boys came to know each other fairly well, a great event occurred. One at a time the members were placed on a stool before the fraternity. Every member was given a chance to tell each man what he thought was wrong with him, what he disliked about him. Some were kind in their objections; at least they wrapped a soft pad around the lead pipe. But others just used the pipe. After that, however, there was little bickering and conflict. The boys got along very well.

But life is not like that. Conflict among clashing personalities arises all through life. There are many reasons, of course. Some people have a martyr complex. They are door mats. They want to be hurt. If there is any shooting they jump up on the ramparts to be shot at, then go around boasting of the wound, as proud of it as a king of his crown, or a hero of his medals.

Others are the bully type. They want to hurt people. Maybe a sorrow, a defeat, or a hurt they have sustained has made them antagonistic toward all people. With brutal frankness they cut and hurt innocent people. Often this arises from an inferiority complex.

There is the person who is allergic to success. He can't stand to see anybody succeed, or to see a movement or organization progress. So long as you are on the losing side he is your best supporter, but start winning—then watch out.

Out of all these sources of conflict arise confusion and misunderstanding.

Dr. Crowe tells of a transcribed radio program. The

beautiful music spoke of love and understanding among men. The speaker's message was a discussion on brotherhood. But the label on the jacket of the record read like this: "Fingerprints will be produced as audible disturbances on this transcription. Please avoid fingerprinting the grooves by handling the record by the outside rim." The author reminds us that this is a parable of life and worship. For the voice of God and the heavenly harmonies may be distorted and marred by minor human disturbances. Petty prejudices, misquotations, harsh words do much to obstruct the kingdom of God. Sometimes they cause a church much concern. The fingerprints of our little differences can mar the heavenly music that God would sound through our souls.

Not only is there conflict with people, but also with nature and the material world. Man has a tremendous task to adjust himself to the physical universe and his environment. There is no rain, and then it rains too much. Drought means long, slow dying. A deluge washes away crops and sometimes cities and people. Cold, snow, and ice come and seem to last forever. And then the sun may come out to scorch and burn for months.

One hot day, when the temperature climbed to 107 degrees, a colored gardener was at work right out in the hot sun. He had mopped perspiration until he could endure it no longer. He took up his handkerchief, mopped his face, laid his hat down, and looked up at the sun and said, "All I'se got to say is, 'Where wuz you las' January?'"

Heat, cold, storm, drought, insects, are all a part of living. The Psalmist called it all ". . . the pestilence that walketh in darkness . . . the destruction that wasteth at noonday." We have to adjust to the material world about us, for it, too, is a world of conflict.

There are certain right and wrong attitudes which we must keep in mind if we are to face up to the conflicts of life and successfully overcome them. First, let us consider some of the attitudes which are harmful in facing conflict. *We ignore it.* We refuse to face the problem before us. Like ostriches we bury our heads in the sand and deliberately disregard one of the real facts of life that should be faced.

We intensify it. When we find conflict we aggravate it. The writer of Proverbs was giving good advice when he said, "A soft answer turneth away wrath, but grievous words stir up anger." Some people go to pieces in a tense situation that demands calm and collective thinking.

Someone has said, "If you can keep your head while others are losing theirs, then you don't understand the situation." We often succumb to that idea.

We Americans need more hearing aids and fewer loudspeakers. We need to be quiet and listen more than we do. Anybody can "pop off," but it takes a real person to face calmly some great issue.

When my wife and I were just children starting out together in the ministry, an eye, ear, nose and throat specialist removed my tonsils. I really had a rough time of it. He requested me to go home and use Aspergum every hour or so. I remember he said to let it trickle down to heal the incision. When we got back to our little apartment we had forgotten what the aspirin product was, but we remembered that it had to trickle down. My dear mate went to the drug store and came back with liquid aspirin. Every hour I let it trickle down my throat. Well, it is largely alcohol and you can imagine what happened. When it reached the incision I felt like the fire-swallower at the State Fair. The doctor got a big kick out of that when I went back to see him. It had not healed but had been aggravated. Some of us are like that in dealing with our problems.

We try to retaliate or get even. That is another wrong attitude about conflict. God said, "Vengeance is mine, I will repay."

A man came to a minister with a problem. He had been involved in a scandal. His wife had forgiven him on his repentance. She had promised to forgive and forget, yet never a day passed but that she reminded him of it. He was tired of hearing about it. She had not kept her word to forgive and forget. The minister sent for her and she said, "Yes, I have forgiven and forgotten, but I don't want him to forget that I have forgiven and forgotten."

But let us now consider the *right attitude toward conflict.* Let me name a few simple but helpful suggestions.

We should strive to remove or interpret conflict. Remove the causes for conflict that can be removed, and try to interpret the cause that cannot be removed. Sometimes there are things which can be done when we face up to our situations. It may require drastic surgery but we see clearly what we should do, and by God's help what we will do. We take action to remove this source of trouble. However, there are times when it cannot be removed; it is a part of our life. It is a burden that we must carry.

Sarah F. Adams had to face the conflict of illness in her family. Her sister's ill health forced Sarah to give up her plans for marriage and accept the rôle of nurse in the home. She interpreted her conflict in the light of God's love and wrote the hymn, "Nearer, My God to Thee." Her faith is so well expressed in the first stanza:

Nearer, my God, to Thee, nearer to Thee!
E'en though it be a cross that raiseth me,
Still all my song shall be, Nearer, my God, to Thee,
Nearer, my God, to Thee, nearer to Thee.

Problems of others may explain their acts and attitudes.
I once knew a man who seemed to change from the good-natured, jolly, soul that he had always been to a crabby, irritable fellow. People avoided him, for often his conversation was colored with cynicism. One day he was being criticized for this change, when a man in the group stepped forward and said, "You fellows don't know that man's problem. You don't know that his wife is ill of a nervous disorder and that after working all day at his job, he often stays up all night with her. I have seen him at two and three o'clock in the morning driving her about the streets of the city. Sometimes she can sleep only when she is riding in the car." Tears came in one man's eyes and he said, "God forgive me for being critical of him and letting him hurt my feelings. I'll bear it from now on if it helps him with his burden."

If we would seek to know "what makes people tick" we might better work with them.

We must resolve the conflict in our own life. If you are constantly in trouble with people, you might take an honest inventory of yourself. Maybe the trouble is with you. Now, most of us would not admit that we are at fault, but it is usually the case. If people are always hurting your feelings or stepping on your toes—if there is always conflict where you are involved—it may be that you have an unresolved conflict in your own life. It is time then to face yourself and try to resolve your own problem.

I knew a woman in another pastorate who came to me with her troubles. Her husband was ill-tempered, she said. The children were cross, and often at each other's throats like cats and dogs. All in her family needed help except her. She went to Florida to spend two weeks with her sister and her home had the first peace in years. The father and children got along without trouble. It was the mother's inner conflict that had disturbed the family relations. We need honestly to face this possibility in our own lives.

We should seek the day of forgiveness and healing. There is nothing better for conflict than forgiveness. It is the healing balm above all others. It is the way that Jesus recommended for getting on with people.

I remember a revival in my boyhood. My home church had not grown for years. It was stymied by deep-seated prejudices, hates, and conflict. Dr. L. D. Patterson came there for a revival. He decided to stay until victory was won. It was the second week before anything broke. Then he had a service of forgiveness. He invited to the front every man who had known enemies but was willing to forgive them. One of the prominent businessmen came down the aisle in tears. He stood there a moment. The atmosphere was charged with excitement. Everyone knew his enemy and of the years of conflict. Would he come? Then he came down. Those men—locked in each others arms—cried away their differences. Then others came and embraced before the altar. It was the change in the life of that church and city. Paul's admonition to live peaceably with all men became a reality to us all. And it can become a reality to your life and mine.

7. THE BATTLE OF LONELINESS

*. . . and yet I am not alone, because the Father
is with me.*   JOHN 16:32.

SOME TIME AGO in a small town in Alabama a neighbor was
invited to join a family in an afternoon ride. They had a
nice, long ride during which the elderly neighbor seemed
really to enjoy herself. She had not been well for some time.
The fresh air, the beauty of the countryside, and the good
fellowship in the car seemed to make a decided change in
her. When they returned to her home to let her out, she
said, "Thank you very much. This has helped me. I guess
my trouble is, I'm lonesome." Now, she is a member of a
noble family which has written its name in the annals of
Alabama in medicine and military life. On the field of battle
from the Spanish-American War down through World War
II that name has been written in heroes' blood. Most of the

family have passed on or moved away, leaving the two sisters. For some months one of the sisters had been visiting in another state, and there in that old, exquisitely furnished family mansion of twenty rooms and four baths the other had lived alone. She diagnosed her case accurately when she said, "I guess my trouble is, I'm lonesome."

Doctors at the Columbia-Presbyterian Medical Center in New York studied 1500 patients suffering from a variety of illnesses and found that an emotional upset lay at the root of more than half of the cases. At Johns Hopkins a doctor examined fifty patients who complained of nausea and found a definite organic reason in only six cases. The rest had literally worried themselves sick. An illustration was that one man's symptoms began the day he lost his job. Loneliness becomes a contributing factor to unhappiness, depression, and finally to physical illness itself.

There are moments of loneliness in every life. William Wordsworth lay bare the human soul when he said, "Points have we all of us within our souls where we all stand single."

Rollo May said in the *Saturday Review,* August 15, 1953:

Whereas the chief problem in Freud's early decades was sexual expression, and the chief problem in the 1930's, when Horney wrote, was repressed hostility . . . there are many indications that we in the middle decades of the twentieth century are moving into an age of loneliness. The barometer portends that if we survive at all we are likely to live in chilly times, when it will be difficult to feel real warmth and meaning in our relation with our fellow man.

The chilly times of loneliness have come or will come to every human being. Why?

There is the loneliness of homesickness. Have you ever been homesick? Well, if you haven't, let me tell you that it is a rough experience.

Dr. Calvin Pinkard of the Trinity Methodist Church of Birmingham, Alabama, and I were in the same cabin in 1951 on the little Canadian Pacific White Fleet liner, the *Empress of France*. We had a cabin mate who was from Scotland on his way to seek his fortune in Canada. As soon as we left Liverpool for Montreal he became deathly ill. We called the ship's physician, who diagnosed the illness as seasickness—probably aggravated by too much spirits on the night before we sailed. For three days and nights that poor fellow stayed in his berth. I was in the berth above him, and often we would carry on conversations during the rest periods. He asked me about prayer. He had strayed away from the upbringing of a good Highland mother. He expressed a desire to return home. One morning as the dawn made its way through the porthole of our cabin I heard my Scotch friend. I looked over at Calvin who was also listening to our friend. It seemed that our talks with him were doing some good. Our friend was kneeling at a chair in the middle of the cabin. He said, "Oh, Lord." Well, that impressed me. I looked over to Pinkard's berth again and he was looking down—smiling. Two Methodist preachers had landed this Scot. Again he said, "Oh, Lord, I'm so seasick I'm about to die." Well, he was sick all right. But it was more than seasickness—he was homesick.

Homesickness, how it cuts the heart. It's a terrible form of emotional illness. The soldier and the student understand, for they have been homesick.

There is the loneliness for companionship. Here we stand

single in a chilly time of loneliness. This is true of people who have a hard time making friends.

Bacon said, "A crowd is not company, and faces are but a gallery of pictures, and talk is but a tinkling cymbal where there is not love."

Long ago the preacher in Ecclesiastes said, "Woe to him that is alone when he falleth; for he hath not another to help him up."

So many people need a little help, a kind word, an expression of interest. We have a tendency to run in little groups and we don't want to take other people in. It isn't that we have anything against them—we just don't know them.

A man stumbled into my study one night just as I was leaving for the evening meal. He said, "I don't have any problem. I've been here several months installing some machinery. I go all over the country, staying about a year in a place. I'm not homesick, I'm used to being on the road; but I guess I'm peculiar and have a little trouble approaching people. I've heard you preach. You seem to be easy to talk to, so I decided to drop around and visit with you a little. You see, sir, I guess I'm lonely."

Young people and childen can be among the worst in shutting people out. A new boy comes to a school and he is neglected, forsaken, and often called all sorts and kinds of names. Sometimes irreparable emotional damage is done. A child draws up into a shell and becomes the bully, the trouble maker. You may say, "Preacher, when are you going to get around to religion?" My friend, I'm talking about the heart of the New Testament—to love the Lord and your neighbor. If you don't believe in a religion that considers other human beings, then you don't believe in the New

Testament religion of Jesus Christ. Many people are lonely for companionship.

There is the loneliness of physical and mental illness. When a man is committed to an institution, whether it be a hospital or sanitarium, he goes into a different world. His normal habits are set aside. He is in bed. His strength limits his activity. He must go by the rules of the institution. He faces the possibility of not getting well. His mind plays tricks on him. This is not an appeal for wholesale visiting in the hospital. That can become a major problem for the patient and the institution. But close friends who do visit should have a delicate understanding of the patient's situation and attitude.

One of the most heart-warming experiences I ever had was in such a case. I had missed a businessman from his office in the town where I was pastor. I had asked, but no one knew where he was. I knew that he was an alcoholic, and I began to wonder. Finally, one day his business partner said, "Preacher, I should tell you where my partner is. He had just gotten to the very bottom of the ladder. He agreed to go to a hospital in South Georgia. No one knows where he is but his wife and me." He told me where the hospital was. I was going down to Daytona Beach in a few days, so I changed my plans and went out of the way for a few miles to see him. When I walked into his room, he was out. I sat down and waited. When he came in and saw me—well, I can't describe it. He had not seen anyone from home in weeks. He threw his arms around me and cried like a child. I must admit that I did the same. An hour's visit with him seemed to make a lot of difference. I know this much—seeing him made my trip better. He was sick in body and mind, he needed a little attention. We should be patient with those who are mentally sick and remember that they live in a different world.

There is the loneliness of old age. People who have been active get on the shelf and become forgotten. Increasingly this has become a major social and psychological concern. By 1960, one-third of our nation will be people over forty-five years of age and one-tenth over sixty-five. Not all of them will be lonely, but some can testify with the Psalmist:

> I look to the right and watch,
>   but there is none who takes notice of me;
> no refuge remains to me,
>   no man cares for me.
>   —Psalm 142:4, RSV.

We have social security and old-age assistance, but they cannot suffice for the needs of the soul. Old people want to be important. They want to be loved.

As children we used to get cross with my grandmother. She was hard of hearing. That is, on some subjects. She might embarrass us by literally shouting to us on the front porch a question about some man and woman walking by in the street, "Who is that long, tall, skinny fellow, and that crazy-looking woman?" We would all, "shoo, shoo" her, but then, when my father was telling my mother some juicy gossip, grandma could be two rooms away and hear every word of it. Yes, we got aggravated sometimes with her, but when she died—we knew that we had lost a trusted friend.

Dr. S. L. Dobbs, father of Bishop Hoyt Dobbs, lived a few doors away from me during my college days. He had been one of the outstanding leaders of Methodism, a man to whom we all owed a great debt; but in his latter days he sat all day alone on his porch or in his living room. Often I would stop by and he would chuckle, "Well, Franklin, in other days preachers and laymen came all day long to talk to me about appointments. They don't come any more." He would hesitate a moment, and then his eyes would twinkle. "Well, there's one thing for sure, son. You come to see me because you want to—not to get something." But he was mistaken—I did go to get something. I went to listen to his stories, to glean from his experience, to sit at his feet.

There is the loneliness of conviction. A man stands single in the chilly atmosphere of a boycott, when his conscience forces him to take a stand for what he believes. Yet we who disagree with him boycott him and make life so very unpleasant.

A man has a right to his convictions. There is a dangerous trend in this country to crucify people who don't agree with the status quo. This nation was founded on free speech, a free press, and a free pulpit. Take them away and you lose your nation.

Some time ago a young Baptist minister was ordered from his pulpit in a Georgia town because of a statement he made on the race question. The people admitted that he was not a radical, that he never had been, and that this statement was sincere and Christian. They also said that they were not too offended over it, but the trouble was, the farmers came in and threatened to quit trading with the members of the congregation if they let this man stay in the pulpit. Because of the loneliness of their conviction, that pastor and his family were moved from that city. This is a deep loneliness that few of us can understand. It is a loneliness akin to that of the great prophets who stand against the tide of popular thinking. And yet if we didn't have people like them, where would this country be?

Time magazine carried an article about a man in England who had to work two years, five days a week, on a job in which no man was allowed to speak to him. He belonged to one union and the men to another. Both were legitimate unions, there was no clash between the organizations, but it boiled down strictly to a matter of jurisdiction on the local level. Yet for two years the fellow workers would not speak to him, answer a question, or return a good morning. That must have been a deep loneliness for the man.

There is the loneliness of disbelief. That cry that echoes and re-echoes down the corridor of the centuries still haunts us, "Oh, that I knew where I might find him." It is the cry of a man who is seeking the face of God, yet is unable to find Him.

It was a lonely night for Simon Peter when he followed Jesus afar off. He had loved Jesus, but had not quite accepted Him in faith as the eternal Lord of life. It was chilly indeed about that fire in the courtyard. Chilly with more than night air—chilly with the deep cold of disbelief. Peter warmed his hands at the fire, but his spirit was not to be warmed until at last he knelt in faith on the shores of the Sea of Galilee, and believed.

It was a lonely night for Judas. He had sold his Lord for a handful of silver. Now he walked into the light of the flaming torches in the Temple. His bloodshot eyes saw only the image of the man who stood there. He screamed, "I have sinned in that I have betrayed the innocent blood," and he ran into the dark and hanged himself. The loneliness of disbelief! Beloved, you can come by faith and drive away the despair of this loneliness.

There is the loneliness of death. We have stood there and watched, but we haven't understood it. The chilly atmosphere of uncertainty.

Nanny Hooper was in her late eighties. She was one of my best friends as well as a loyal member of the church. She sent for me one day. When I got there she was seated before the fireplace sewing a dress. She said, "Pastor, I am making my shroud. I wanted to make it with my own hands. Don't be alarmed, I'm not a sick sentimentalist, I'm not going to cry. You see, Pastor, it's like this. I've always made my party dresses. I've never trusted the seamstress for that. Back when we used to have big events here, gala occasions, I always made my own dress. And now that the biggest celebration of all is coming up, well, I want to make my own dress. It will be glorious, to go into His presence, to see my husband, the father of these fine children of mine; to see many old friends who have gone on, and to see, above all, Jesus my Lord. Oh, no, pastor, I'm not dreading it; I'm looking forward to that party. I wanted you to know." It didn't happen until after I had moved, but one day they told me that Nanny was gone, and I thought, "She's gone to the big party that she's been expecting." It was not a lonely path for her.

Whatever our problem may be, whether homesickness, loneliness in sickness, old age, conviction—we can say this, "I am not alone, because the Father is with me." The words of Jesus offer us assurance as we live in these days.

8. A CURE FOR TROUBLED HEARTS

Let not your heart be troubled: ye believe in God, believe also in me. JOHN 14:1.

Casting all your care upon him, for he careth for you. I PETER 5:7.

WHEN I WAS thinking one day about the broken hearts of today, a picture came to my mind which I had not thought of in twenty-five years. In 1931 I was a trombonist for the East Alabama Vagabonds, and I remember a picture on a sheet of music that we played. The scene depicted a girl seated on a window seat surrounded by boxes and bundles of remembrances. There were old love letters tied together with ribbons. There was an old doll and several empty candy boxes. In the middle of them was a big valentine

heart, which was torn right down the middle. Some of you
will be able immediately to name the song and you will
be right—"I've Found a Broken Heart Among My Sou-
venirs." There was always a note of pathos about that song.
Somehow, it seemed to strike at the heart of one of the
most trying of human problems, the problem of a broken,
aching heart. In the song, the girl's trouble came out of a
broken love affair. Others come from loneliness, broken
health, disappointment, defeat, and loss of loved ones and
friends. Does Christianity have anything to say about this
problem?

Are we like Humpty Dumpty? "Humpty Dumpty sat on a
wall; Humpty Dumpty had a great fall; all the King's horses
and all the King's men cannot put Humpty Dumpty together
again." Is a broken heart like that? Is there no balm in
Gilead? Is there no healing for broken hearts?

In a short story entitled, *Pastoral Symphony,* Andre Gide
tells of a lovely young girl, Gertrude, who had been blind
from birth. Her blindness actually caused her to be pro-
tected from life to the extent that she had a childlike senti-
mental picture of the people around her. One day she
underwent an operation, and her eyes were opened. Two
things immediately impressed her. One was that nature was
more beautiful than she had ever imagined; light and color
fascinated her. The other was that the faces of people were
sadder than she had expected; almost every one of them
was lined with anxiety, care, and inner restlessness. She
almost wished her eyes had never been opened. Is this all
that life has to offer?

One can almost hear the faint voices of a far-away choir
singing the Negro spiritual:

> Nobody knows the trouble I'se seen.
> Nobody know but Jesus.
> Nobody knows the trouble I'se seen,
> Glory, Hallelujah!

Jesus knows. He walked this lonesome valley and He walked it by Himself. He discovered broken hearts and had His own broken by rejection, rumor, hate, suspicion. Even on the cross He shed both water and blood; the writers called it the evidence of a broken heart. Just before His death He said, "Let not your heart be troubled: ye believe in God, believe also in me." Peter, who knew Him as few did, said, "Casting all your care upon him, for he careth for you."

We have established our premise—that ours is a world of broken hearts, of troubled hearts, and, moreover, that our God offers healing. Let us now be as practical as possible in seeking to analyze our situation. At this point let us look at some suggestions offered by Dr. E. Stanley Jones.

It is necessary to start with the negative in order to reach a positive conclusion. There are some *don'ts* which are very important in dealing with broken and burdened hearts. If you should go through a physician's clinic, he would sit down with you after the full report had come to his desk and point out to you some of the things you should not do. They are just as important as the things you should do. There is a place for the negative in healing of souls just as there is a place for the negative in the healing of bodies. Let me enumerate some important don't's:

Don't think your case unique. Name your trouble and you will find somebody down the hall or across the street with the same trouble. It is strange indeed how many people have the same troubles. You have some rare disease that you have never heard of before and you will discover scores of people who have had or seen it.

A number of years ago I came back from Palestine with some rare disease and had to have an operation. (Now, I have wanted to tell you about my operation but until now I haven't had the faintest chance to get it in.) After I had been in the hospital several weeks, a woman slipped past the nurses and the "no visiting" sign one day and came into my room. She was a bearer of good tidings—or was she? She said that she lived near the hospital and had heard of my rare disease. She had had it herself and wanted to comfort me. She said, "Now, don't get too worried. The worst hasn't come yet." She went on to say, "You will have convulsions, and matters will go from bad to worse. I know, because I've been through it. They carried me to Johns Hopkins, Mayo's, out to a clinic in Texas. I nearly died— then I started to get well. You'll make it, but you've got to get lots worse yet." She was most consoling!

It is important to know that every day people are facing troubles like yours and are winning. For centuries men have coped with trouble and there seems to be no turning point. The fellowship of suffering is a brotherhood with steel bonds.

Don't give yourself to self-pity. Once self-pity sets in, one turns to the seclusion of an introvert and sorrow becomes a festering sore. There are certain wounds which the physician will not allow to close until healing has set in. The physician keeps them open for drainage until they are ready to close. Spiritual wounds may heal on the surface, but self-pity causes them to fester underneath. Spiritual infection brings despondency, bitterness, and unbelief.

In a certain community in which I used to live was a big

house on a once well-known estate. In other years crowds
had come to the lakes for swimming and picnics. It was a
busy estate and an equally busy household. Then death
had struck. The blinds were drawn, the doors locked, the
lakes neglected. Inside lived a maiden lady with her sorrows.
She feared people. She wanted to be let alone. The beauty
which she had once known left her soul. Self-pity had
taken its toll.

Don't retail your troubles. There is no spiritual therapy
like talking. We make a mistake when we believe that we
should keep our troubles shut up within us. It is good to
talk to someone about them.

When I returned home after my father's death, my brother
said to me, "Don't let mother talk about daddy—it isn't
good for her." I answered, "Brother, you are wrong there.
A certain amount of talking is necessary." I let mother talk
to me about daddy and it did her good.

But I have said that in order to say this. There is a difference in sharing and retailing our troubles. Sharing is done
with friends. Retailing is telling everybody. When people
think of us they must not associate us with trouble, unless
it be with the mastering of trouble. The definition of a bore:
"A person who talks about his rheumatism when you want
to talk about yours."

When our son was about four years old he was tussling
with his uncle and had a fall. He complained of pain, so the
doctor put his arm in a splint. That went on for days. Everyone asked about the arm. He kept it in the sling. It was the
center of conversation. Finally, we decided that he was retailing his troubles. We had the arm X-rayed, and no
trouble was found. Then the arm was taken out of the
sling, and things became normal again. Trouble can become

the center of our lives. We can unconsciously thrive on it and live by it.

Don't resign yourself to trouble and don't fight against it. This sounds like a paradox, but it is not. Resignation to trouble means complete defeat at its hands. It means capitulation. Yet God has given us the mind, strength, will and other supports with which to overcome. On the other hand, there is the tenacious fighting spirit that pounds its head against a stone wall. There are some things we cannot change. We must live with them. Somewhere there is the delicate balance of seeking to work out that which is workable and to accept that which we cannot change.

I am sorry that we had to start with the negative, but it was necessary in order properly to establish the positive side. In seeking a cure for broken hearts we must remember some positive thoughts. There are some *do's* as well as *don't's* in this problem of living.

If trouble has come, try to determine whether or not you are the cause. This is important. Some of our trouble comes from our own sins and wrong attitudes.

In an earlier pastorate was a young man who came to me often. Everybody was wrong but him. The mill company had bad policies. The superintendent was a tyrant. The overseer in his shop was guilty of favoritism. His own fellow workers were slovenly and jealous. The neighbors were the wrong kind of people. Rent was too high, pay too low. The schools were foul, and he could learn nothing. Society was generally rotten. This country itself was going to pot. One day when he came in to see me I said, "Tom (we'll use that name), what I am going to say is going to make you mad. You have attacked everything and everybody but me, and after what I say you'll attack me too, for I'm getting into the arena. Have you ever thought about the fact that some of this trouble is with you?" Oh, yes, I made him mad. He turned and stalked from my office. And what a hot letter he wrote me. I kept it for a number of years, so that when I began to feel too proud of myself I could get it out and read it. That boy told me exactly what he thought of me in no uncertain terms. But let me tell you this. Later he apologized to me and thanked me for saying what I had said. Today, that boy is one of the most successful businessmen in his community.

Some of our trouble is with us. Sometimes it is our sins. "For the wages of sin is death. . . ." Sin is a terrible thing. There are clean and unclean troubles. The unclean come from sin. We need surgery. We need the Divine Surgeon to operate. We need His blood to cleanse. A man who has been unfaithful to his wife cries, "Why do I have so much trouble?" And a man given to excessive drink cries, "Why do I have so many troubles?" Let the X-ray of God be turned on your spiritual tissue to see what is there. It could be that our own sins dog us. But, on the other hand, many of our troubles cannot be laid to our sins. The Old Testament view that all trouble came from one's sins was repudiated by Jesus. Some of the best people seem to have the most trouble. They are not at all to blame. Let us remember it has been said, "The saints suffer most." But in case some sin is involved, let us be sure to face ourselves first before we face our troubles.

Determine to make your trouble make you. Someone has said, "When fate throws a dagger at you, there are two ways to catch it: either by the blade or by the handle." Trouble makes us or breaks us. It sweetens us or embitters us. It strengthens us or weakens us.

There is a famous statue in Mexico by Jesus Garcia entitled, "In Spite Of." The sculptor lost his right hand in the
midst of his work on the statue. He was determined to
finish it, so he learned how to carve with his left hand.
Actually, his work with the left hand seemed better, and
in it all he discovered a quality of life which he had not
known before. They called the statue, "In Spite Of." The
sculptor let his trouble make him.

I have been to the Louvre twice and each time there are
two works of art that I look on with increasing apprecia-
tion—"The Venus of Milo," and the "Winged Victory."
Both are superb works of art, but the remarkable thing is
that both are severely mutilated. The arms and part of the
robe are gone from the "Venus," and the "Winged Victory"
is headless and her clothing torn. Yet, strangely enough, in
no way have these mutilations impaired the beauty of the
statues. Rather they seem clothed with the spirit of eternity.
They speak of perfection and breathe of beauty. They have
suffered, but have endured. The marring has added to their
beauty.

A recent letter from Marilyn Terry, a missionary in
Taejon, Korea, has a story that I must share with you. On a
hill in the city are located two Methodist schools—a Kinder-
garten Training School and a Bible Training School. On a
high spot between the two schools a chapel is being built.
Dr. and Mrs. W. E. Shaw of the Methodist Mission there
are sponsoring the chapel as a memorial to their only son,
Bill Shaw, who gave his life in the Korean War while serving as a marine. Bill grew up in Korea, a son of missionary
parents, and came to America to study to be a missionary
to Korea. When the war started, he had such deep convictions about it that he volunteered as a marine and was killed

in Korea. His wife and two children in Ohio plan to go to Korea, where she hopes to serve as a missionary. The Shaws are using all the money they can find to build the chapel in memory of their son. A Korean man, who is not a Christian, is giving part of the land for the chapel because he has heard of Bill giving his life for his Korean friends. The parents, too, are making great sacrifices for the chapel. The loss of their only son has not caused them to quit. Rather they have used it to make them—and to make the society around them—better.

One evening at the Quarterback Club in our city someone announced his regret that Charlie Boswell was not able to be present. When Charlie Boswell is absent he is missed. This famous University of Alabama football player, who lost his sight during the war years, has developed a beauty of soul that blesses everyone with whom he comes in contact. He has determined to make his troubles make him.

Is there a cure for troubled hearts? There is. Finally, above all, it rests on Jesus. In Him we may find the strength to win this battle. Without Him it will probably be a losing fight. He said, "Let not your heart be troubled: ye believe in God, believe also in me." In Him we find the mender of broken hearts, the healing balm for the soul, a cure for the troubled hearts of these days.

III. GOD IS THE ANSWER TODAY AND ALWAYS

9. *KEEPING GOD AT THE CENTER OF THESE DAYS*

. . . for I know whom I have believed. . . .
II TIMOTHY 1:12.

DR. DANIEL POLING, editor of the *Christian Herald,* relates an experience he had with his son, Clark. Clark Poling was one of the four chaplains who went down with the troopship *Dorchester* off the coast of Greenland in the early days of World War II. The four chaplains—two Protestants, a Catholic, and a Jew—gave their life belts to others and, holding hands together on deck, went down with the ship. This story of heroism swept America, and the Federal Government issued a special stamp with this scene pictured on it. Dr. Poling tells of the turning point in his son's life. The lad, a teen-age boy, was in prep school in the upper part of the state. One day he called his father on long distance, saying that he had to see him. Said he, "Dad, it's very important. Don't tell mother that I'm coming. Meet me at the station. I've got to see you." The father said he tried to imagine what kind of trouble the boy had gotten into. He could hardly wait for the train to arrive, and was at the depot when the boy got off. Clark was disturbed; his father could tell that. Instead of boxing his Dad as he usually did, or picking him up and kissing him, the lad merely extended his hand. They got in the car and drove to the office. The father locked the door and Clark slumped over in the chair near the desk. He buried his face in his hands. The father waited anxiously for the boy to begin. Then, like a bolt of lightning from the sky, it came. Clark lifted his tear-stained eyes and said, "Dad, what do you know about God?" Dr. Poling was caught off balance. He had not expected this question and had no prepared answer. He just spoke right out of his heart. "Son, I don't know much about God. I don't know much about God, but what I know I really know. I have tested Him in joy and in sorrow, in victory and in defeat. Son, I don't know much about God, but what I know I really know." That day Clark Poling made his decision for God and started down the road of service which, as a chaplain, led him to the supreme sacrifice aboard the *Dorchester*.

Dr. John Redhead, of Greensboro, North Carolina, tells of a recent visit to the campus of a college during religious emphasis week. He met with the officers of the student association to ask their advice concerning themes for his message. They gave him only one suggestion. They said, "We feel a sense of unreality in our religious life. Please tell us how to find God real."

People who come to my office for counsel and guidance often express the same thing. Some time ago a man said to me, "I know how to run my business. I'm not doing a perfect job of it, but in my line I think I operate about as efficiently as anybody in my city. I know how to make money. I know how to get along with my family. I know how to keep friends. But concerning the most important thing in the world I am ignorant. I don't know anything about God. Will you please help me to know God?"

We may be familiar with many subjects, and yet if we do not know God we are ignorant and unlearned. We may master our field of business, medicine, law, teaching, or skilled labor, but if we do not know God we have failed miserably to acquire the truth.

When Robert Browning was questioned about his deepest conviction expressed through his poetry, he was quick to answer, "I am very sure of God."

Paul was one of the best trained men of his day. A product of the university town of Tarsus, he came to Jerusalem to study in the school of Gamaliel. You had to be a Phi Beta Kappa of that day to worm your way into this very select group, which came from all over the Mediterranean world to sit at the feet of this great teacher. Paul's writings reveal one of the best minds ever known to Christendom. Yet this great thinker, philosopher and student, said, ". . . I know whom I have believed, and am persuaded that he is able to keep that which I have committed unto him against that day." He said, "I *know.*" There were no reservations, no question marks, no loopholes. Paul was sure of his knowledge of God.

I stood in Rome in the quiet yard of the Church of Three Fountains. Tradition tells us that Paul was imprisoned and beheaded on this spot. I went down into the dungeon where he spent his last hours, where, probably, he wrote, "I am now ready to be offered, and the time of my departure is at hand. I have fought a good fight, I have finished my course, I have kept the faith: Henceforth there is laid up for me a crown. . . ." "I know whom I have believed." The smooth stone and sword used to behead him—in their glass case— did not spell tragedy to me. They sang a song of victory. For this man had gone into eternity with conviction in his heart. He knew God. *Do you know Him?*

Do you know Him as a pre-eminent God? Does He have first place, or have you mixed Him up with a lot of false gods in the hopper of your life?

To many of us God makes no difference. Some years ago a cartoon appeared in *Collier's* magazine depicting a couple sitting dumbly in the kitchen. The cartoon carried a title which could not easily be forgotten, "We ain't interested in nothing." How true this is of many people! They eat to live and live to eat. Time is heavy on their hands. The fact that this great world is filled with beauty and misery, living and dying, hope and despair, does not concern them at all. Religion is merely some dressed-up affair that has to do with old churches, stuffy ritual, and bells ringing on Sunday morning. These people are not opposed to God, but neither are they for Him. It just doesn't make any difference. In the nature of things God cannot endure this indifference. He must be pre-eminent.

Isaac knew where God belonged in the scheme of things. When he moved his flocks, herds, servants, and household to a new area, this great giant of faith put God first. In the new land he first erected an altar to God, and all fell down in worship. Then the servants erected the tents for Isaac's family. Finally, they dug wells for the animals. God first, home second, and business third. "But," you say, "Isaac didn't face the sort of competition that a man faces in this day." Are you sure of that? Isaac faced the possibility of being attacked by lurking animals. He faced the demands of nature. The cattle were almost dead of thirst. Sometimes wells did not produce water and the efforts to dig them were in vain. But Issac always knew that God should be first. He knew that even business problems would work out better when God was in on them. So the first thing Isaac did was to build an altar to God.

Dr. Albert E. Cliffe, famous Canadian chemist, tells us in his book, *Lessons in Living*, of a discovery he made. As a student of diet he was greatly distressed to find that people who ate the proper foods were suffering from diseases which, according to the principles of nutrition, should never have occurred. Dr. Cliffe then turned to a study of the mind, and came to the conclusion that the food we feed our minds every hour and every day is of far greater importance than the food we put in our stomachs. The lack of mental vitamins are often the real cause of sickness. This great scientist learned that although we must not minimize the importance of the principles of bodily nutrition we must also give proper regard to the principles of spiritual nutrition. That is where God comes in. To be a strong, vigorous, happy person, one must know God, and God must be pre-eminent in life.

Do you know Him as a forgiving God? What do you know about God's forgiveness? We are all sinners. We have fallen short of the glory of God. We are undone. We can never know God fully until we come to Him in confession of our sins, and witness His cleansing power. We need not be afraid to come, for He has said, ". . . him that cometh to me I will in no wise cast out." ". . . though your sins be as scarlet, they shall be as white as snow. . . ." "If we confess our sins, he is faithful and just to forgive us our sins. . . ." Dr. Norman Vincent Peale once made a valuable suggestion that two collections should be taken everywhere in all churches on Sunday morning. The first should be the regular financial offering. The second would be different. The members of the congregation would be asked to write on a card their worries, fears, guilts, and sins. They would not need to sign their names, for God would recognize them, anyway. The ushers would then pass the plates and the minister would receive the cards, take them to the altar, and solemnly give the people's troubles and sins to God. For in Christ He has forgiven us. In the words of the hymn, "He has covered them all, He has covered them all . . . and that means me." My sins were covered by His blood. When I come to know God in the relationship of forgiveness, then it is that I know His true love for me.

Once, when Dwight L. Moody was holding a meeting in St. Louis, he preached on the Philippian jailer. The next morning the local paper covered the meeting under the rather sensational headline—"How the Jailer of Philippi Was Caught." A notorious criminal named Valentine Burke sat in his cell and casually glanced at the paper. The headline caught his eyes, for he had once been in Philippi, Illinois, and thought the jailer there to be in some sort of trouble. He read the story and got the gist of the sermon. As he thrust the paper aside in disgust, Moody's text kept coming to his mind, "Believe on the Lord Jesus Christ and thou shalt be saved." Moody used it nine times in that sermon. He related how forgiveness had come to the jailer. At midnight Valentine Burke prayed for the first time in his life. Forgiveness came. God appeared in all His glory. The prison was transformed into a room of heaven.

The sequel to the story is most interesting. Burke was released from prison, and the warden had him shadowed. After all, he was a notorious repeater, and all this stuff about religion could be a blind. Burke went to New York and sought honest employment. He frankly told his story of crime and forgiveness to every prospective employer, but no one believed him. He could not find a job anywhere. Through all this, though, he remained straight. Finally, he drifted back to St. Louis. The warden sent for him and asked what he had been doing since his release. He related his story. The warden said, "You are absolutely right. I was impressed by you, and I've had detectives follow you to see if you were giving me the straight of it. You have lived a good life. I need another deputy and I am offering you the job." Burke lived the rest of his life there in St. Louis. He had learned something about God that so many people overlook—forgiveness. Burke was an upright man and a trusted employee. Do you know God in the full pardon of your sins? If not, today is a good time to accept Him and learn of Him.

Do you know Him as a sympathetic God? Is He a God seated on the rim of the universe far removed from your problems and burdens? What do you know about His sympathy and understanding?

Eighteen centuries ago there lived a man named Marcion who felt that the God of the Old Testament was not a sympathetic God. The wars, the slaughter, and some of the old laws of men dealing with men disturbed him. So he solved the problem by deciding that the God of the Old

Testament was altogether different from the God of the New Testament. He persuaded many to follow him in abandoning the Old Testament altogether.

Dr. E. Stanley Jones tells of a mother who was reading about the slaughter of the Amalekites to her little daughter. The child was disturbed. She couldn't understand how God would approve a thing like that. Her mother explained that people in that day didn't know as much about God as we know today, for we have Christ, who explained God to us. The little child smiled and said, "Oh, yes, mother, now I see. All that happened back there before God was a Christian."

God had always been a Christian in that His love, His sympathy, and His understanding were always existent, but it was not until Christ came to reveal God to us that we really came to understand Him ourselves. Through Christ we have learned of God's tender compassion. We have found God approachable, merciful, and full of love.

A few years ago, a businessman told me a story as we flew out of New York. He had suffered a great loss in the death of his father. As an influence and a guiding light his father was next to God in his life. His father's death had so deeply wounded him that for a time he even doubted his faith. One day he decided to have it out with himself. He was on a business trip for his company and drove out of his way to the village where his parents were buried and where he was reared. Since the death of his father, he had purposely avoided the home town. He drove through the streets of the sleepy village to the cemetery beyond. He parked his car and slowly made his way through the gate and over across the cemetery to the little mound where his father rested. He sat down beside the grave. The tears came. All of his burdens became heavy on his shoulders. Resentment welled up in his heart. Then he seemed to feel a hand on his shoulder. He looked up. No one was there. He bent his head again, and again felt that hand on his shoulder. He said it felt so warm and comforting. He waited. He seemed to hear a voice, "My son, my son, weep no longer, your father was a good man. He is with me now. He is better off than you are. I understand your sorrow, because I have suffered, too. When my children suffer, I suffer also. Grieve not, my son. All is well." A long time passed. The man sat there in a sort of unexplainable ecstasy. When he stood to go, the memory was still fresh, but the burden was gone. Peace had come. For he had found the reality of a God who was sympathetic and understanding.

What do you know about God, beloved? Do you know Him as a *Pre-eminent God?* Do you know Him as a *Forgiving God?* Do you know Him as a *Sympathetic God?* What do you know about Him? He is available to us all. It behooves us to seek Him and try His ways. And St. Paul's victory will become our victory, too. We can join Paul in saying, "I know whom I have believed." We can keep God at the center of these days.

10. LOVE IS THE GREATEST FORCE FOR ANY DAY

And now abideth faith, hope, love, these three;
but the greatest of these is love.

I CORINTHIANS 13:13.

A NUMBER OF years ago I made my first visit to Chattanooga, Tennessee, and to Lookout Mountain, where the Battle of Chattanooga was fought on November 24, 1863. There General Hooker and his Federal troops captured the ridge held by General Bragg's men of the Confederacy. My grandfather had fought in that engagement, and I was interested in every word the lecturer said and in every detail explained. There in a gift shop I found a little, most unusual whistle. It had a little peep hole, through which one could look and view a tiny picture of the battle. It was entitled, "The Battle Above the Clouds." In later years, when my mind went back

95

to the battle for Lookout Mountain's ridge, the great tides of blue and gray beating against each other, the belching of cannons and the staccato sound of musketry, I thought of another battle above the clouds. It was fought on a little mound outside the gates of an ancient city. The only sounds of battle were the groans of dying men on their crosses or the outbursts, now and then, of the crowd who mocked and cursed them. That day great issues were fought out; great forces came together in such a mighty clash that the world is still reverberating from the impact. It was on that mound that they crucified our Lord in the greatest battle known to mankind.

Between Milton's poem, "On the Morning of Christ's Nativity," and the sonnet, "On Shakespeare," you will find his poem entitled, "The Passion." Having written of the incarnation and the temptation, it was Milton's purpose to write on the atonement, the great work of Christ on the cross. But the poem had just eight introductory stanzas, and at the end of the eighth stanza is this note, "This subject the author, finding it to be above the years when he wrote it, and nothing satisfied with what it was begun, left it unfinished." If so great a genius and intellect as Milton found that the cross was too great a theme for him, then what shall this minister say about it? The best we can do is to touch the hem of the crimson robe of the atonement.

Calvary was a battle of far greater proportions than the human mind can comprehend. Here love and hate wrestled for mastery. Here righteousness and unrighteousness struggled for victory. Here condemnation and salvation fought for the prize. The battle was for the hearts of nations and for the souls of the individual men of this globe. To speak

on each phase of this great struggle would be impossible
in one or even many sermons. I want to lift up only the one
struggle, that between *love* and *hate*.

This is an age-old struggle. Since Cain's jealousy of his
brother Abel turned into hate and climaxed in murder, men
and nations have had a difficult time.

Hate is not born in us; we acquire it. The dog and the
cat are reared together in the same house and sleep in the
same box. They acquire hatred for each other only as certain developments take place in the house. Children of
different races and classes love each other and like to play
together until they hear enough from their families to create
a dislike which may finally grow into hatred.

*If only we could find the answer to hate, we could solve
the problems of war.* For we know that since early man war
has always been the product of hate. One tribe would
resort to war to wrest hunting grounds from a neighbor.
So, also, suspicion of another tribe would bring about fear
and hate. A feeling of insecurity because of the plots and
plans of a neighboring tribe would generate hate. Even
simple dislike could grow into hate. One tribe would dislike
the philosophy, color, or religion of another, and animosity
and hate would be the result. The same may be said of
nations today. Jealousy, envy, suspicion, fear, and dislike
breed war.

*If only we could find the answer to hate, we could also
solve the problem of the "isms" which plague man.* Nazism
and communism both have an answer in this issue of love
versus hate. Where communism breeds on class hatred and
economic division, it cannot stand before the power of love.

Justice William O. Douglas tells of sitting one night at

the Officers' Club in Leh. They were talking about communism. Said Mr. Douglas, "Communism professes love for mankind, but it preaches hate and practices terror. People want love and affection. It will be love and affection, not physical power, which will finally win Asia."

Some time ago, a Paris newspaper, writing of the great issues faced by mankind, said, "An English periodical notes that the word 'atom' was defined in four lines in an encyclopedia dated 1768, while the article on love was five pages long. The new edition of the same encyclopedia has five pages on the same subject of the atom but not a word about love." Maybe this is the heart of our problems in the world today.

If only we could find the answer to hate, we could solve the problems of human relationship. Here we can dig deep into personality problems of frustration and fear, knowing that our religion has an answer.

Dr. Ernest Logan, an Irish Presbyterian minister, tells of an experience in Dublin. Sometimes he stood on the bridge of a tugboat with a captain friend as the latter performed his duties in the harbor. Very often, when the tug passed a certain lighthouse a siren would sound. The minister asked if a silent watcher set it going as the tug passed. But the captain said that no one lived in the lighthouse. He pointed to a Coast Guard station on shore and explained that it was controlled from there. He said, "An electric beam is focused from that Coast Guard station on the lighthouse. On foggy days the little particles of water hanging in the air break the beam. As soon as the beam breaks, the siren automatically sounds every few seconds." The minister looked at the blue sky and the shining sun. There was no fog, yet the siren was sounding. When he called this to the attention of the captain, the captain said, "The little particles of soot and dirt from our smokestack keep breaking the beam. That is why the siren is sounding." So it is in life. Our little petty annoyances, frustrations, jealousies, doubts, fears, resentments, all bring unhappiness and hatred to poison our hearts and break the beam of our relationship with God and our fellow men. Let me illustrate with the following:

Some time ago a nationally known minister was telling us of an experience he had with a boy. This lad was working for a woman sixty-five years of age. She scolded him about something and he turned on her and beat her nearly to death. The judge of the juvenile court called the minister. He told the minister that not in all his career had he seen a case exactly like this. He could not get through to the boy. There was a barrier. The minister went to see the lad, and then out to the apartment where he lived. The grandmother and two unmarried aunts lived there together. They had reared the boy, but had resented the burden of caring for him. They had slapped him about and cursed him all his life. In the boy's heart a burning hatred for them had been built up. When the woman, who was about the age of his grandmother, scolded him, he transferred his hatred for his grandmother to her and almost killed her. The minister took a great liking for the boy. It required almost a year to penetrate the shell the boy had built about himself, but a steady flow of love did it. His life was changed by love.

A Cleveland minister, traveling on a train, went into the diner for his evening meal. The dining steward placed him at a table with another man, where he saw a folded newspaper. He reached for it, when the other man said abruptly, "That belongs to me." Soon a waiter came with some orange juice, and the man asked gruffly, "Did you strain it?" "No,

sir," was the answer. "Then take it back, I have ulcers and
can't drink it unless you strain it." The minister ventured a
question, "Sir, may I ask, do you have ulcers because you
are cross, or are you cross because you have ulcers?" The
man replied, "Well, if you are so nosy, ask my doctor." Then
the man looked at the minister and asked what his business
was. When the minister told him he laughed sarcastically.
"What is your business?" asked the minister. "Making
money," came the gruff answer. "How do you make it?"
the minister inquired. "Any way I can," boasted the man.
To make a long story short, some weeks later this man sent
for the minister. He was sick in body, mind, and soul. The
minister learned the trouble. Twenty-two years before, the
man's wife had run away with another man, leaving her
husband with their three children. For twenty-two years he
had snapped at men, not because he had anything against
them, but because he hated his wife, and his hatred had cut
the beam to God and man. He lived on an island in his
soul. A long process of love freed him from hostility and
changed his life.

Yes, if we could find the answer to hate, we could solve
the problems of war, of "isms," and of human relationships.

Love is the most powerful force known to mankind. Paul,
writing to the church in Corinth, speaks of love, "Though
I speak with the tongues of men and of angels, and have
not love, I am become as sounding brass, or a tinkling
cymbal." He ends the chapter, "and now abideth faith,
hope, love . . . but the greatest of these is love."

Professor Sorakin, probably the most outstanding sociolo-
gist of this modern era, tells of his escape from Russia during
the revolution. He was a professor in the university in what

was then St. Petersburg. He believed in freedom from the czars but not in the evils which succeeded them. Three times he was imprisoned by the Bolsheviks. Three times the love of a friend opened the prison doors for him to escape. He says that on a tree somewhere in the Soviet Republic of Georgia is carved a sentence which he put there before he fled the country. It reads, "Love is the only way."

Dr. Roy Burkhart and his wife spent one evening with us a few months ago. He is pastor of the well-known Community Church of Columbus, Ohio, which has a membership of 5,200 and a large staff of workers and ministers. He is the modern apostle of love. Time and again he said that love was the most powerful force in the universe. He told us of planting corn in three pots as an experiment. The same seed, soil, and sunshine were given each. One pot was hated, one was neglected, and the third was loved. Everyone who passed participated in the experiment by cursing the first pot, neglecting the second, and loving the third. The first withered, the second was anemic, the third blossomed forth. Said Dr. Burkhart, "Even a plant is subject to the power of love and the power of hate."

There is an old poem in English literature, "Love Among the Ruins." It depicts a young couple meeting amid the ruins of an ancient castle. As they hold hands there the author sees it all clearly. The tyrant is gone. His castle now crumbles. The road which knew his chariot is covered with growth. But love remains. Love is best.

The cross of Christ is love's pardon for man's redemption from sin and hate. Hate thought it had won on Golgotha's heights in the long, long ago, but it was wrong. Love won that day.

It was love that took my place on the cross of Calvary,
It was grace, redeeming grace, that paid my ransom, full and
    free;
Over sin, without, within, I have the victory,
Through grace, marvelous grace, that lives in me.*

Christ's love was manifested in the cross. It is the great plus sign of man's salvation. It is love revealed in forgiveness.

Recently I read a story that I had not heard since my boyhood. The writer said he was on a train, and became interested in a young man across the aisle from him who seemed highly nervous. He engaged the young man in conversation and obtained his story. It seems that when he was a boy he ran away from home. He had not communicated with his parents for years, and had heard from an indirect source of their bitterness concerning him for leaving home and neglecting them. He had written them after all those years, pleading for forgiveness. He told them he understood their reasons for feeling hurt at his neglect, and said that if they would forgive him and let him come home again, to put a piece of cloth in the old apple tree near the railroad tracks. If he saw this sign in the tree when the train passed he would know that he was forgiven, and would be welcomed, and loved again. As the train drew near the farm, the man became more apprehensive. He peered out the window. "We are very near my father's place now, but they can't forgive me; they won't, I've mistreated them, I've wounded them." He held his breath. The train rounded the curve. He leaned over and looked hard. Then he literally

* From "Love, Mercy and Grace," words and music copyright 1938 by Rodeheaver Company, owner. International copyright secured. All rights reserved. Used by permission.

shouted, "Not one flag, the whole tree is full of flags." Forgiveness was written all over the tree with every sheet, handkerchief, tablecloth and pillowcase the family owned spread on its branches. Love had triumphed. That is the story of the cross. The Battle Above the Clouds saw love defeat hate, and bring redemption to us all. Love was the greater force then. Love is the most powerful force for the living of these days or of any day.

11. THE BELL OF HOPE SHALL RING AGAIN

> *... and ye shall be witnesses unto me both in Jerusalem, and in all Judaea, and in Samaria, and unto the uttermost part of the earth.*
>
> ACTS 1:8.

SHORTLY AFTER World War II a popular novel, *A Bell for Adano*, by John Hersey, swept America. It was the story of an American unit's experiences in attempting to bring order out of chaos in an Italian village and restore it to normalcy. The first committee of local citizens to call on the American commander did not request food, medical supplies, or materials to patch up their war-torn homes. Their request was very strange indeed. They asked the commander to get a bell for their church. When the tides of war swept through, their bell had disappeared. It had been their

105

inspiration, the symbol of all their hopes and dreams. Now it was gone. Nothing else really mattered any more. They wanted a bell for Adano. After many difficulties, the Americans were able to find a bell. When the villagers heard the bell ring, joy came again to Adano. Order was restored and hope shone again in their eyes.

Let me tell you a counterpart to this story. The setting is in Cuba, Queen of the Antilles. I heard the story when I was serving in one of the missionary campaigns there. Years ago there was a small Methodist church in Abreus, a community located near Cienfuegos. Since the church was small, it had no resident pastor. The custom in Cuba is for the pastor to get to the church when he can, and ring the bell to notify the countryside that services will be held in an hour. I have gone with Cuban preachers into villages to hold services where the preacher had not been for a month. The church bell would say, "The pastor is in town and will hold services one hour from now." That was the purpose of the bell in Abreus. Twenty years before, a cyclone swept through this village and destroyed the church. In Abreus were two sisters named Valero, devout Christians and members of the church. After the tragedy they gathered up all they could find of their beloved little church—a couple of small benches, a communion set, the pulpit Bible, and the bell from the tower. These they took to their home and guarded with care. "We shall not die," said the sisters, "until we hear the bell ring again from the church tower." Years later a Methodist missionary came to Abreus. He visited the sisters and heard how they prayed daily and worked to hear the bell again. They told him that they would not die until the bell rang again in a new church tower. He became interested in the rebuilding of their church, and wrote letters to the States about it. He visited among the people of the village and stirred up interest. Only a few of the old members remained, but they renewed their endeavor to build a new church. He made the prayer of the sisters his prayer: "O God, let me live long enough to hear the bell ring from the church tower." On February 10, 1955, Bishop John Branscomb, Methodist Bishop of the Florida-Cuba Area, and Dr. Harry Denman held services of dedication in the beautiful new church in Abreus, and at the close of the services they rang the bell. The people wept for joy. Everyone wanted to pull the bell cord, so each was given the privilege. And that is the story of a "Bell for Abreus."

The Book of Acts records the ascension of Jesus. Forty days after the Resurrection He called His disciples together and spoke His last words to them. He told them to tarry in Jerusalem until they received power from heaven. Then He said, "But ye shall receive power, after that the Holy Ghost is come upon you: and ye shall be witnesses unto me both in Jerusalem, and in all Judaea, and in Samaria, and unto the uttermost part of the earth." "Go ring the bell of good tidings to the world," He said. Men had longed to hear the bell. They were challenged to go ring the bell of hope in a world of despair; the bell of light in a world of darkness.

Through the years, the church bell has become a bell of freedom. Wherever men have heard it they have been free, or struggling with some hope against the opponents of freedom. Wherever it has been silenced men have been enslaved. Go into any country in the world and listen for the church bells on Sunday morning. They will tell you more than bales of reading material, government decrees, and even the talk of the people on the streets.

Democracy is dependent on religion. We need to burn that thought into our hearts. Democracy does not exist in nations where the worship of Almighty God is not accepted. The countries of the East, such as India, have been greatly influenced by Christianity. The closest friends of Mahatma Gandhi noticed the influence of the Christian movement on him. The same may be said for Nehru. The worship of God has played a part in making men free. The exponents of regimentation know that if they can silence the church bells they can control the conscience of a nation.

The life of Martin Neimoller, a German submarine commander in World War I, who became a minister of the gospel, is part of the story of the Nazis' struggle with the church during the days of Hitler's rise to power. As a matter of fact, according to Dr. Neimoller, Hitler was never able completely to bind the churches. He was afraid to do so. He knew the army would rebel. He tried by subtilty to have ardent anti-Nazi ministers replaced with neutral ones. He never won completely the battle against the church bell —symbol of freedom. It would be an amazing story to most of us to see the freedom the church yet has in East Germany under the Russians. There is a constant struggle to keep the pulpit free and the bells ringing. Our Christian forces are not losing ground; they may even be making some progress in this battle.

A few months ago the papers carried the story of the death of Miss Annie Wheeler in a Richmond, Virginia, Hospital. I shall never forget the time when I became acquainted with this great soul. I was holding services in Courtland, Alabama, and asked the pastor about the possibility of our going to the Wheeler plantation. He explained to me that visitors were no longer allowed there, but that he knew

Miss Annie personally and would call her. She invited us to come out. We spent the afternoon with her there on the Wheeler plantation. She showed us the relics of her father, which she had carefully preserved. Among them were his saddle and several uniforms. There was the uniform he wore when he harassed Sherman. His forces were the only forces to interfere with Sherman's march to the sea. "Fighting Joe" Wheeler was one of the greatest men of the War between the States. Then there was his blue uniform which he wore in Cuba in the Spanish-American War. He was the first high ranking officer of the former Confederacy to put on the blue again. For this he was severely criticized. Miss Annie Wheeler spoke of it the afternoon we visited her. Her eyes flashed when she told the story. Said she, "He was not a traitor to the things for which he fought in the War between the States. He died believing them, but he also believed in the freedom of this country and of men everywhere. When freedom called him, he went." The bell of freedom has long called noble men and women to live and die for the principles of true liberty everywhere.

When World War II ended with the official surrender of the Japanese, a great wave of excitement swept this nation. In our cities and towns we understood we were to ring the church bells when the news came. We had a tremendous bell in the tower of my church, which could be heard for miles. I was just waiting for the opportunity. For hours we listened to the radio. Then came the good news—the war was over. I ran to the church vestibule to ring the bell, but before I could get there I heard its clear tones. A war wife who had waited two years for her husband to come back from overseas had gotten there ahead of me. With tears streaming down her cheeks, she was pulling away, and her little boy, who couldn't remember what his daddy looked like, was pulling, too. It touched my heart. This was the bell of freedom. Under God this nation was safe and free.

There is a quartet number which one sometimes hears over the radio in parts of the South. It says, "Joy bells are ringing down in my heart."

Wherever the Gospel of Christ is preached, the joy bells ring. Jesus sent His disciples into the world to tell the good news of freedom, but also to relate the good news of joy. The Angel of Bethlehem had opened the first chapter of the Christian story with the words: "Fear not: for, behold, I bring you good tidings of great joy, which shall be to all people." This was a message of joy to the world. Christ's witnesses have this story to tell in every land and clime, that Jesus rings the joy bells in the soul.

St. Cyprian, in the third century, wrote a friend:

This seems a cheerful world, Donatus, when I view it from this fair garden, under the shadow of these vines. But if I climbed some great mountain and looked out over the wide lands, you know very well what I would see. Brigands on the high roads, pirates on the high seas, in the amphitheatres men murdered to please the applauding crowds, and under all roofs—misery and selfishness. It is really a bad world, Donatus, an incredibly bad world. Yet, in the midst of it I have found a quiet and holy people. They have discovered a joy which is a thousand times better than any pleasure of this simple life. They are despised and persecuted, but they care not. They have overcome the world. These people, Donatus, are the Christians and I am one of them.

One day, when Robert Browning was sitting at his desk, his wife softly slipped up behind him and placed a manuscript in his jacket pocket. Elizabeth Barrett Browning fled up the stairs, while her husband read some of the most beautiful words ever written by a woman to her life's mate. Hidden in the sonnets she gave him those famous lines:

> The face of all the world is changed, I think,
> Since first I heard the footsteps of thy soul.

Here the inner joy bells were ringing, for love had caused them to ring out their tidings of happiness. That is the kind of joy that comes to the hearts of those who follow Jesus. It is not a surface thing made up of noise and shouting. It is a quiet, peaceful tide moving through the soul.

Have you lost your joy? You may have it again if you will come to Jesus.

An Italian lad had molded some beautiful bells. The work of his hands had given him fame throughout all Italy, and his bells had been mounted in the tower of the monastery of his city. Then came war, leaving destruction and death in its wake. When the villagers returned, the bells were gone from the tower of the monastery. The lad started out in search of them. From one city to another he traveled, listening to the bells. The years passed and age crept upon him. Still, he had not found his bells. Finally, one evening he was aboard a ship coming into the harbor at Limerick. He heard bells in the city. He listened. It was the music of his bells. No others in the world were like them. Their music wafted him back to the land of his birth and work.

Come back to Christ, and hear the joy bells again. They are your bells. You may hear them. Wherever the Word of God is carried, men hear them and are made happy.

The disciples were commanded by Christ to witness in Jerusalem, Judæa, Samaria, and the uttermost part of the earth to the salvation which was available for all men. This is the heart of the missionary message.

A terrible disaster took place in the mines of a German community. The company's whistle told the story of tragedy. Anyone who has ever lived in the mining district knows the sound of that whistle and the stark fear that seizes the people. Wives and children rushed from their cottages to the entrance of the shaft. Emergency crews hustled by with their equipment. Several men were trapped by a cave-in. Deadly gases were seeping through. The men had to be rescued. Tents went up to dispense food and coffee. Emergency telephone lines were laid. Tired, dirty miners came and went with their equipment. They were fighting tons of rock and they were fighting the clock. The men below were breathing their last oxygen. Time was running out. The signal, if the men were found alive, was to be the ringing of the church bells. Hours passed. People stood around and talked at the shaft or whispered softly behind the closed doors of their cottages. Crews came and went. The deadline for the safety of the men was past. Could there be a soul alive now? Then suddenly they heard it. The church bells were ringing. People rushed from their cottages. A mighty chorus went up to God. One could hear it for miles around in the quiet valleys. They were singing that old German hymn:

> A mighty fortress is our God,
> A bulwark never failing;
> Our helper He, amid the flood
> Of mortal ills prevailing.

That is the message of the bell of Salvation. A mighty fortress is our God. Come in and find comfort and shelter.

The bell rang again in Abreus, Cuba. Its joyous notes told men that freedom, joy, and salvation belonged to them. In home, hamlet, city, and across the mission fields the church bell tells the story today. *The bell of hope shall ring again.*

12. THESE DAYS AND THE DAYS TO COME

> *Brethren, I count not myself to have apprehended: but this one thing I do, forgetting those things which are behind, and reaching forth unto those things which are before, I press toward the mark for the prize of the high calling of God in Christ Jesus.*
>
> PHILIPPIANS 3:13-14.

SEVERAL YEARS AGO I sailed from Europe for America on the American-Hamburg ship, *The Hamburg.* It was a slow boat, taking more than eight days for the crossing. I remember well the terrible fog which engulfed us the second day out. The ship literally crept through the encircling gloom of it, with the foghorn blasting every minute or two. My cabin mate and I were in a small cabin down in third class,

115

right at the waterline and in the very bow of the ship. My berth was situated where I could put my hand against the thin steel skin of the ship and feel the vibration of the water against the outer surface. During that terrible fog my roommate and I had a conversation. We were in our berths listening to the foghorn and thinking about the ship moving through the gloom without seeing ahead. A remark was made to the effect that if we hit something our cabin would be crushed like an eggshell. Then my roommate made a thought-provoking remark. He said, "That doesn't bother me in the least. We're in the hands of the Lord on land or sea, so I'm going to take a nap." The snores which came from the berth below assured me in a few moments that he was practicing what he preached. Those words, simple yet profound, have stayed with me through the years —"That doesn't bother me in the least. We're in the hands of the Lord on land or sea, so I'm going to take a nap."

What did the fog-bound waters of the North Atlantic hold for us? No man could answer that question. But every man could answer one question for himself, Have I enough faith to relax in the Lord and trust myself to His tender care?

One of the most famous stories with a tantalizing ending is *The Lady or the Tiger?* by Frank Stockton. A youth, who was bold enough to seek the affection of the king's daughter, was condemned to open one of two doors. Behind one was a beautiful girl, whom he must marry, and behind the other, a tiger. The king's daughter learned the secret and signaled her lover to open one of the two doors. But which? That is where the story ended. The future was never explained.

Dr. Ashley Chappell was one of the greatest storytellers of the Southland. Civic clubs were glad to pay him a nice

fee for their Ladies' Night program. Several times, as a
pastor or civic club member, I had the privilege of inviting
him to my town. One year he was invited to address the
State Convention of the Lions Club in Alabama. The District Governor of the Lions was greatly pressed for time, and
he made it a point to emphasize this in his introduction of
Dr. Chappell. He said, "Dr. Chappell, we are paying you
fifty dollars to speak to us thirty minutes, not thirty-two
or thirty-five, but thirty." The crowd roared but the famous
preacher-humorist was not to be outdone. He spoke for
twenty-eight minutes, then took out his watch and said, "I
have one more story to tell you. When I was pastor in Texas
a rancher member had a big wedding for his daughter. The
setting was the flower garden of the ranch, which was
exquisite beyond description. The guests came from far and
near to witness the ceremony. I stood before the bride and
groom and asked the question, 'If any man knows any im-
pediment whereby these two may not be lawfully joined
together, let him speak now or forever hold his peace.' At
that moment two men stood. On one side a tall oil man got
up and pointed his rifle at us, and said, 'I have a reason,
doctor.' On the other side a cowboy stood, cocked his pistol,
and said, 'I have a reason, doctor.'" At that moment Dr.
Chappell hesitated, looked at his watch, and said, "Gentle-
men of the Lions Convention, I have spoken my thirty
minutes as requested by your governor. I will now take my
seat." People started popping up all over the place. They
shouted, "Finish your story! Finish your story!" Dr. Chappell answered, "No, my time is up." One man got up and
shouted, "Mr. Chairman, I move that we extend the time
and give this man another fifty dollars to finish that story."
They never knew what happened, for Dr. Chappell didn't

finish the story. Life is like that. We know the story to this point, the present. We do not know what lies ahead.

Sometimes I think it is well that we don't know. If someone really knew the future, we would pay him a large sum to tell us, and then we would be unhappy about it.

Several years ago a younger preacher friend who had started out under my ministry came to visit us. The first thing he said was, "While I'm here I want to see Mrs. So and So, the famous fortuneteller who lives near here. While I'm here in this part of the state I want to see her. I am interested in psychiatry and in her uncanny ability to foretell the future. I understand you know her well." To which I answered, "I do. When I was a boy her husband was one of my father's best customers. I have visited in her home and have been a guest there while holding services in her community. She is a member of the Board of Stewards of our little church there. She will not tell fortunes on Sunday. She tithes her income, and will not take money unless the visitor is satisfied with the interview." My young friend said, "I am dying to see her." We drove over, and found her seated on the porch. She was a very gracious person and offered us the hospitality of her home. When I told her what my friend wanted she refused at first. He insisted, so, finally, she took him into the interview room. When he came out his eyes were as large as saucers. When we drove away he told me, "She said I would have a bad automobile accident during the next eight or nine months." "Do you really believe it?" I asked. His teeth chattered, and he answered, "I don't know." Well, for a year he was about the most careful driver you ever saw. He lived in fear of an automobile. He did not have an accident. We think we want to know the future—but do we?

What lies ahead—sickness, death, suspense, accidents, tragedies; or victory, great opportunities, high privileges, great honors, good health and happiness? Who knows? The best we can do is to follow the advice of my cabin mate, put ourselves into the hands of God, relax with confidence, and do our best to live successfully in these days.

Paul had an excellent way of stating it: ". . . this one thing I do, forgetting those things which are behind, and reaching forth unto those things which are before, I press toward the mark for the prize of the high calling of God in Christ Jesus."

There are some things I can do to help with the future. I cannot know what the future holds, but I can do my part to help. Attitudes are important factors in co-operating with God in any day.

I shall have less hate and more love. It will definitely help me with my future if I can keep down inner tensions and conflicts with people. At the best, some tensions and conflicts will come along. I would not be so absurd as to suggest that a person can live completely free of misunderstandings, dislikes, and tension. You cannot make everybody like you. Some people will dislike you because most people like you. Some human beings are allergic to popular people. The popular doctor, the well-liked political leader, and the business establishment with a good reputation are all avoided by such people. And you can't keep people from misinterpreting what you have said. That is a part of living. You can, however, control your feelings toward them. You and I will not be judged for the other man's attitude toward us, but we will be responsible for the way we have reacted to it. He may hate us or dislike us, but we do not have to hate or dislike him. The world needs a little bit of love.

A young German woman who suffered under the Nazis described the effect that Hitler had on German youth. They were hungry for love. Hitler said, "No one loves you—I love you; no one will give you work—I will give you work; no one wants you—I want you." They were hungry for it and they followed him. If an earthly man, sinful and selfish, will give his followers a stone for love, what may we, with the help of our heavenly Father, give? The world is hungry for love. Whatever your field of work, if you love your employer more, or your employees more, it will help. If you can love your fellow workers more it will have its effect. Our lives—whatever comes—will be richer, sweeter, purer, and we will take it in stride better, if we love.

I shall have less fear and more faith. W. H. Auden has called ours the "Age of Anxiety." Albert Camus calls this "The Century of Fear." Fear is a terrible thing. It takes something out of life, and involves the whole being.

When Reverend L. W. Tubbs, former pastor of the First Methodist Church, Phenix City, Alabama, was our speaker at First Methodist Church in Gadsden, some months ago, he spent the night at the parsonage. The whole nation has read the Phenix City story of crime and chaos. My guest sat in the living room, relaxed, with the shades up. Said he, "This is wonderful, to be able to be seated in your living room with my back to an open window. How wonderful to go to bed with a sense of security." I questioned him and he told me how they were afraid to sit near a window during the early weeks of the clean-up. People who were involved in the crusade would always draw their curtains and sometimes turn out the lights. When the children were out at night in the car the parents lived on pins and needles until they came in. He told of telephone calls all night, and when one would answer all he heard was a deep breath or a low curse. He said that people couldn't stand that indefinitely. Fear disturbed digestion, sleep, and clear thinking.

Fear taken into the future will become heavy baggage. It will destroy the joy of the journey.

Let me illustrate. Have you ever come to a crossroads while on a journey in some unknown area? You studied the roads and then chose one of them. But every yard along the road chosen by you was one of misery. Your fears caused you to miss the beautiful scenery along the way. The lake covered with water lilies could have been a mud hole so far as you were concerned. The field of mellow grain was no more than a murky bog. You drove on every moment a moment of despair, until you stopped for directions. When the farmer said, "Yep, you're on the right road," that brought back the sunshine and the beauty of the scene. The skies came alive with color, the landscape too. Fear had vanished, faith had come. Decisions are like that. Did I make the right decision when I signed that contract? Is that the best school for my child, or have I wrecked her life by letting her go there? Was that the right investment? Did I do the best by changing jobs?

I heard the story of a plumber whose fears and anxieties got the best of him. He was in bed with the flu at the time of a big freeze in the city. The afternoon after the freeze had thawed a little the calls of his patrons started coming in. He received ten calls, and some fifty burst pipes were reported. The poor fellow got his pencil and tablet and started figuring. If ten homes have fifty burst pipes, that is five broken pipes to the house. There are approximately a million homes in the city; that means that five million pipes are broken. And that means that the plumbers of this city will have to work all the year, under houses in the cold mud, fixing pipes. The plumber became temporarily insane.

I shall have fewer cares, more confidence. The future for us will be much better if we can keep the little cares of the world from getting us down, and can determine the right values. With these values we can go into the future with more confidence.

A short time before he was killed in a London air raid, Lord Josiah Stamp, one of the great financial authorities of the twentieth century, gave an address over the B.B.C. dealing with standards of money. He concluded his remarks by saying: "Before I finish I should like to say something, and it is this—I have not the smallest interest in what I have been talking about tonight, not the slightest interest in this or any other scale of values except it accord with that other scale of values introduced into this planet by Jesus of Nazareth. This is the one and only scale of values that really matters and which no man listening to my voice can ever afford to ignore without peril to his soul." This great financier went down to the very heart of a major problem—the cares of money and earthly values. Eternal things count more. If only we can believe that as we go into the living of these days and the days to come.

In the life of Peter Marshall, *A Man Called Peter,* written by his wife Catherine, an experience is recorded in the last chapter which those who have read the book will not soon forget. The famous young pastor of the New York Avenue Presbyterian Church in Washington had suffered his second heart attack. An ambulance was called to remove him from his home to the hospital. Mrs. Marshall had to remain at home with their son, and did not go to the hospital that night. As Peter was being carried through the front door on the stretcher he looked up to Catherine's face and said, "Darling, I'll see you in the morning." She didn't know that night that those would be Peter's last words to her, but after it was all over she weighed those words. That is one of the most radiant expressions of the Christian faith ever spoken. That is what Christ really said in the Upper Room long ago, "I'll see you in the morning." What confidence it gives us as we go into the future. I can walk by faith and not by sight. I can have the blessed assurance that I will be with my Lord and that I shall see my loved ones on that eternal morning of the soul. In that faith cares mean less and confidence more.

We do not know what the future holds for us. We cannot comprehend it. But with less hate and more love, less fear and more faith, less cares and more confidence, and with our hand in the hand of God, we can go forth rejoicing in these days and in the days to come.

Date Due

BROADMAN
B P
SUPPLIES

Code 4386-04, CLS-4, Broadman Supplies, Nashville, Tenn.,
Printed in U.S.A.